The Tragedy of
Macbeth

Editors:

MAYNARD MACK
Sterling Professor of English, Yale University

ROBERT W. BOYNTON
Former Principal, Senior High School,
and Chairman, English Department, Germantown Friends School

THE TRAGEDY OF
MACBETH

by William Shakespeare

Edited by

Maynard Mack and Robert W. Boynton

BOYNTON/COOK PUBLISHERS
HEINEMANN
PORTSMOUTH, NH

BOYNTON/COOK PUBLISHERS
A Division of
HEINEMANN EDUCATIONAL BOOKS, INC.
361 Hanover Street   Portsmouth, NH 03801
Offices and agents throughout the world

The figure "The Globe Playhouse, 1599-1613, a Conjectural Reconstruction" is reprinted by permission of Coward-McCann, Inc. from *The Globe Restored: A Study of the Elizabethan Theatre,* Second Edition, by C. Walter Hodges. Copyright © 1953 and 1968 by C. Walter Hodges.

Library of Congress Cataloging-in-Publication Data

Shakespeare, William, 1564-1616.
   [Macbeth]
   The tragedy of Macbeth / by William Shakespeare ; edited by
Maynard Mack and Robert W. Boynton.
      p.   cm.
   Summary: Presents the play with an introductory essay putting the
play into its historical context and discussing its themes; a note
on Elizabethan theater; and concluding commentary and study
questions.
   ISBN 0-86709-021-9
   [1. Shakespeare, William, 1564-1616. Macbeth. 2. Shakespeare,
William, 1564-1616--Study and teaching. 3. Plays.] I. Mack,
Maynard, 1909-   . II. Boynton, Robert W. III. Title.
PR2823.A2M34 1990
822.3'3--dc20   90-31129
                                                CIP
                                                AC

Printed in the United States of America

92 93 94   5 4 3 2

PREFACE

The Mack - Boynton editions of Shakespeare offer the plays most widely studied in schools and colleges, in a format designed to be read more easily than the normal pocket-sized editions, yet inexpensive, durable, and, more important, informed by the best in modern Shakespeare scholarship. The plays included in this series are judiciously framed with supporting material, enabling the reader to deal creatively with the text in the classroom, in small groups, or independently.

The editors of this series have founded their work on the following principles:

(1) Reading Shakespeare is not a poor substitute for seeing Shakespeare well performed, but rather a different arena of experience with its own demands and rewards.

(2) Seeing and hearing the language of the play in the theater of the mind is central to the experience the playwright provides.

(3) Knowing something of the characteristics of Shakespeare's own theater lessens the danger of asking the wrong questions about the structure and meaning of his plays.

(4) The text should be as faithful as possible to the most authoritative early edition, with a minimum of editorial interpolation.

(5) Notes and glosses should explain and not simply suggest, but at the same time readers should be granted their common sense and their mother wit.

(6) Commentary before and after the play does not detract from direct experience—is not intrusive—if it suggests ways of approaching the text that allow the reader a broader range of imaginative involvement.

(7) Questions on the text provoke further questions and provide deepened insight if they are not used or thought of as prodding or testing devices.

Each volume in the series contains an introductory essay which briefly puts the play in its historical context (not because our interest is in theatrical history, but because the play *has* a historical context) and discusses the play's themes and concerns and how Shakespeare went about dramatizing them. Along with the introductory essay is a brief note about the Elizabethan theater, a conjectural reconstruction of the Globe Playhouse, and a general note on the policy of this series with respect to texts, with specific reference to the play in hand.

Following the text there is a commentary on how to approach the play as a live dramatic experience in the theater of the mind. Observations on the imaginative world of the play in general lead into discussions of selected scenes, the intention being to place the sometimes narrow interests of academic Shakespeare study in a context that gives scope to the whole personality of teacher and student and calls up sense and feeling as well as idea and theme.

Also included in the material following the text are questions, specific and general, on the play, some brief information about Shakespeare himself, a chronological listing of his works, and suggested basic reference books, recordings, and films.

CONTENTS

INTRODUCTION

i

Macbeth is a play with many faces. Seen in one light, it appears to be simply the brutal story of a Scottish usurper, whom Shakespeare had read about in one of his favorite sourcebooks, Raphael Holinshed's *Chronicles of England, Scotland, and Ireland.* Holinshed's Macbeth is an arresting figure, not so much because of his murderous career, which seems to have been only a little in excess of the habits of his time, as because he is said during his first ten years of rule to have "set his whole intention to mainteine justice," and during his last seven years to have begun to "shew what he was, instead of equitie practising crueltie."

Shakespeare, though no historian, knew that no man wears a mask of virtue for ten years, only to reveal that he was "really" a butcher all along. This oddity in Holinshed's conception may have challenged him to speculations that ended in a conception of his own: that of an heroic and essentially noble human being who, by visible stages, deteriorates into a butcher. The great crimes of literature, it has been well said, are mostly committed by persons who would ordinarily be thought incapable of performing them, like Brutus in Shakespeare's earlier tragedy, *Julius Caesar,* or Raskolnikov in Dostoevsky's *Crime and Punishment.* The hero that Shakespeare draws in *Macbeth* is no exception. At the beginning of the play, even the thought of murder stands his hair on end, makes his heart knock at his ribs (I iii 147-48). By the end, he is too numb to care. His wife's death scarcely stirs him, and the wild cry of her women in their grief only reminds him of what he can no longer feel:

> The time has been my senses would have cooled
> To hear a night-shriek, and my fell of hair
> Would at a dismal treatise rouse and stir
> As life were in't. I have supped full of horrors.
> Direness, familiar to my slaughterous thoughts,
> Cannot once start me. (V v 10-15)

ii

Coming at the play from another angle, we realize that its medieval story of the rise and fall of a usurper has been colored by, and also in some sense mirrors, a number of contemporary interests and events. In 1605, for instance, just a year before the probable date of the play's composition and first performance, came the revelation of the Gunpowder Plot, a plan to blow up King, Lords, and Commons in Parliament as they convened for the new session of that year on the fifth of November. The plot was made known through an anonymous letter only ten days before the intended massacre, and the climate of shock and suspicion that prevailed throughout England, especially London, immediately thereafter has almost certainly left its mark in the play's haunted atmosphere of blood, darkness, stealth, treachery, and in the vividness with which it communicates the feeling that a whole community based on loyalty and trust has been thrown into terror by mysterious agencies (both unnatural and natural) working through it like a black yeast. Several of the conspirators were from Warwick, Shakespeare's own county, and may have been known to him. If so, there was no doubt personal as well as dramatic relevance in such observations of the play as Duncan's "There's no art/To find the mind's construction in the face" (I iv 13-14), or Macbeth's "False face must hide what the false heart doth know" (I vii 92). At the very least, such statements, however they were meant by their author, would have held an exceptional charge of meaning for the play's first audiences in 1606.

iii

Witchcraft, too, is among the contemporary interests that the play draws into its murderous web. Witchcraft was a live issue at all times in the 16th and 17th centuries, but it loomed especially large in the public mind after the Scottish James I came to power, following the great Elizabeth, in 1603. James considered himself an authority on witches, had published a book on demonology in 1599 affirming their existence and their baleful influence in human affairs, and, in 1604, a year after his accession to the throne, inaugurated new statutes against them. Thus, the whole topic was accentuated at just about the time of the writing of the play.

Except in one phrase (I iii 7) and in his stage directions, Shakespeare always refers to the witches in *Macbeth* as *weyard* —or *weyward—sisters*. Both spellings are variations of *weird,* which in Shakespeare's time did not mean "freakish," but "fateful"—having to do with the determination of destinies. Shakespeare had met with such creatures in Holinshed, who regularly refers to the supernatural agents with whom Macbeth has dealings as "the three sisters," or "the three weird sisters," i.e. the three Fates. The witches in the play, however, are by no means so unambiguously defined. They have considerable power of insight and suggestion, we gather, but they do not determine a man's will, and Macbeth never blames them for influencing what he has done, only for tricking him into a false security. They are presented to us, moreover, in a climate of suggestion that is fully as demeaning as it is aggrandizing. If they belong with one part of their nature to an extra-human world of thunder, lightning, rain, and demonic powers (I i), and, as Banquo says, "look not like th' inhabitants o' th' earth" (I iii 42), they have nevertheless some of the attributes of defeminized old women (I iii 46-48), their familiar demons assume shapes no more terrible than those of cat and toad (I i 9-10), and the actions with which they identify themselves—killing swine, wheedling chestnuts, and persecuting the "rump-fed ronyon's" sea-going husband (I iii 1-30)—show a pettishness and spite that seem perhaps more human than diabolical.

On the other hand, the weyard sisters are obviously more impressive than the ordinary garden variety of 17th-century witch, the village crone or hallucinated girl, and their collusion with such dire agents as Lady Macbeth invokes in I v (44ff) and Macbeth in IV i (50ff) seems unmistakable. The obscurity with which Shakespeare envelops their nature and powers is very probably deliberate, since he seems to intend them to body forth, in a physical presence on stage, precisely the mystery, the ambiguity, the question mark (psychological as well as metaphysical) that lies at the root of human wrong-doing, which is always both local and explicable, universal and inexplicable, like these very figures. In their relations with Macbeth, they are obviously objective, "real" beings with whom he talks. Yet they are also in some sense representative of potentialities within him and within the scheme of things of which he is a part. What is emphatically to be noticed is that the weyard sisters do not suggest Duncan's murder; they simply make a prediction, and Macbeth himself takes the matter from there. The prediction they make, moreover, is entirely congenial to the situation, requires no special insight. Having made himself in this last battle more than ever the great warrior-hero of the kingdom and its chief defender, what more natural than that the ambitious man should be moved in the flush of victory to look ahead, hope, imagine? Hence, while recognizing the objectivity of the sisters as the Devil's agents, we may also look on them as representing the potentialities for evil that lurk in every success, agents of a nemesis that seems to attend always on the more extreme dilations of the human ego.

iv

Besides the lore of witchcraft, in which he was intensely interested, and the great Plot which threatened to destroy him together with his Parliament, James's own tenure of the English throne seems to be celebrated, at least obliquely, in Shakespearc's play. His family, the Stuarts, claimed descent from Banquo, and it is perhaps on this account that Shakespeare departs from Holinshed, in whose narrative Banquo is Macbeth's accomplice in the assassination of Duncan, to insist on his "royalty of nature" and the "dauntless temper of his mind" (III i 56-58). Many critics see a notable compliment to James in the dumb show of kings descending from Banquo ("What, will the line stretch out to th' crack of doom?" IV i 128) which so appalls Macbeth at the cave of the weyard sisters. Some commentators, influenced by its Scottish background and its use of a story involving one of James's reputed ancestors, go so far as to suppose that the play was actually composed for a royal occasion and conceivably by royal command. What is certain, in any case, is that the playwright has effectively transformed a remote and primitive story into a theatrical event tense with contemporary relevance. The almost routine assassination of a weak, good-natured king in Holinshed becomes, in Shakespeare's hands, a sensitive and terrifying exposition of the abyss a man may open in himself and in the entire sum of things by a naked act of self-will.

v

This brings us to the third face of *Macbeth,* its character as parable, as myth. For all its medieval plot and its framework of Jacobean feeling, the play has a universal theme: the consuming nature of pride, the rebellion it incites to, the destruction it brings. In some ways Shakespeare's story resembles the story of the Fall of Satan. Macbeth has imperial longings, as Satan has; he is started on the road to revolt partly by the circumstance that another is placed above him; he attempts to bend the universe to his will, warring against all the bonds that relate men to each other—reverence, loyalty, obedience, truth, justice, mercy, and love. But again, as in Satan's case, to no avail. The principles his actions violate prove in the event stronger than he, knit up the wounds he has made in them, and combine to plunge him into an isolation, or alienation, that reveals itself (not only in social and political but also in psychological terms) to be a kind of Hell. As Milton's Satan was to put it later, in *Paradise Lost:* "Which way I fly is Hell; myself am Hell."

In other ways, the story Shakespeare tells may remind us of the folktale of which Marlowe's *Dr. Faustus* is one version: a man sells his soul to the Devil in return for superhuman powers, only to find in the end that his gains are illusory, his losses unbearable. It is true, of course, that Shakespeare's hero is attracted by the Scottish throne, not by magic or by power in general; and it is likewise true that he signs no formal contract like his predecessor. Still, the resemblances remain. Macbeth does open his mind to diabolical promptings:

> This supernatural soliciting
> Cannot be ill, cannot be good.
> If ill, why hath it given me earnest of success,
> Commencing in a truth? I am Thane of Cawdor.
> If good, why do I yield to that suggestion
> Whose horrid image doth unfix my hair
> And make my seated heart knock at my ribs
> Against the use of nature? (I iii 142-49)

He imagines himself, moreover, to have received immunities of a superhuman sort:

> I will not be afraid of death and bane
> Till Birnam Forest come to Dunsinane. (V iii 67-68)

> But swords I smile at, weapons laugh to scorn,
> Brandished by man that's of a woman born. (V vii 16-17)

And he finds in the end, like Faustus, that his gains amount to nothing:

> I have lived long enough. My way of life
> Is fall'n into the sear, the yellow leaf,
> And that which should accompany old age,
> As honor, love, obedience, troops of friends,
> I must not look to have; but, in their stead,
> Curses not loud but deep, mouth-honor, breath,
> Which the poor heart would fain deny, and dare not.
>   (V iii 24-30)

The very immunities he thought had been guaranteed him prove deceptive, for Birnam Wood comes to high Dunsinane after all, and so does an antagonist not born of woman in the usual sense. In the end, Macbeth knows that what he had begun to fear after Duncan's murder, in the course of meditating Banquo's, is true: he has given his soul to the Devil to make the descendants of Banquo, not his own descendants, kings. All his plans have become instrumental to a larger plan that is not his:

> They hailed him father to a line of kings.
> Upon my head they placed a fruitless crown
> And put a barren sceptre in my gripe,
> Thence to be wrenched with an unlineal hand,
> No son of mine succeeding. If't be so,
> For Banquo's issue have I filed my mind;
> For them the gracious Duncan have I murdered,

Put rancors in the vessel of my peace
Only for them, and mine eternal jewel
Given to the common enemy of man
To make them kings—the seeds of Banquo kings.
(III i 66-76)

vi

As Freud noticed long ago, the two Macbeths complement each other in their reactions to the crime. Her fall is instantaneous, even eager, like Eve's in *Paradise Lost;* his is gradual and reluctant, like Adam's. She needs only her husband's letter about the weyard sisters' prophecy to precipitate her resolve to kill Duncan; within an instant she is inviting murderous spirits to unsex her, fill her with cruelty, thicken her blood, convert her mother's milk to gall, and darken the world "That my keen knife see not the wound it makes" (I v 44-56). Macbeth, in contrast, vacillates. The images of the deed that possess him, simultaneously repel him (I iii 146-54, I vii 1-25). When she proposes Duncan's murder, he temporizes: "We will speak further" (I v 79). Later, withdrawing from the supper they have laid for Duncan to consider the matter alone (I vii 1-28), he very nearly decides not to proceed. It takes all her intensity, all her scorn of what she wrongly chooses to call unmanliness, to steel him to the deed. Throughout this first crime, we notice, it is she who assumes the initiative and devises what is to be done (I v 68-78, I vii 68-79). Yet we would certainly be wrong to see her as monster or fiend. On the contrary, she is perhaps more than usually feminine. She is conscious of her woman's breast, her mother's milk (I v 51-52); knows "How tender 'tis to love the babe that milks me" (I vii 60); and, when she thinks to carry out the murder herself, fails because the sleeping King too much reminds her of her father (II ii 14-15). We may infer, from this, that she is no strapping Amazon; Macbeth calls her his dearest "chuck" (III ii 52), and she speaks, when sleep-walking, of her "little hand" (V i 45). Thus such evidence as there is all suggests that we are to think of her as a womanly woman, capable of great natural tenderness, but one who, for the sake of her husband's advancement and probably her own, has now wound up her will almost to the breaking point.

An equally important contrast between the two Macbeths appears sharply in the scene following the murder, one of the most powerful scenes that Shakespeare ever wrote. Their difference of response at this point is striking—not only because he is shaken to the core and cannot conceal it, whereas she shows an iron discipline throughout, but also because his imagination continues as in the past to be attuned to a world of experience that is closed to her. That world is visionary and even hallucinatory, we can readily see, but at the same time, it is the mark of a keener moral sense, a fuller consciousness of the implications of what they have done, than she possesses.

The difference between his and her responses is related to a form of double vision that extends throughout the play. Shakespeare establishes for us from the beginning one perspective on his story that is symbolic and mythical, a perspective that includes both the objective weyard sisters, on the one hand, and the subjective images of horror and retribution that rise like smoke from Macbeth's protesting imagination, on the other. He also establishes, as a second perspective, the ordinary world of Scotland, where Duncan is king, Macbeth becomes king, Malcolm will be king, and the witches are skinny old women with beards. In general, Macbeth enacts his crimes in the historical world, experiences them in the symbolic world, and out of this experience, new crimes arise to be enacted in the former. To put it in different terms, a force that seems to come from outside the time-world of history impinges on history, converting history into an experience for Macbeth that is timeless and mythical. We are asked to sense that his crime is not simply a misdeed in the secular political society of a given time and place, but simultaneously a rupture in some dimly apprehended ultimate scheme of things where our material world of evil *versus* good and virtue *versus* vice gives way to a spiritual world of sin *versus* grace and hell *versus* heaven.

vii

The suggestiveness of Shakespeare's play in this larger sense is electric and inexhaustible. Every element it contains lives with a double life, one physical, one *meta*physical. Consider night, for instance. Night settles down half way through the first act and stays there through much of the rest of the play: I v-vii, II i-iv, III ii-v, IV i, and V i are definitely night scenes, and several more, undetermined in the text, could be effectively presented as such, e.g. III vi, IV ii-iii. All this is ordinary nighttime, of course, but it is obviously much more. "Thick," "murky," full of "fog and filthy air," it entombs "the face of earth" (II iv 10), blots out the stars and the moon (II i 1-7), "strangles" even the sun (II iv 8). Duncan rides it to his death, as does Banquo. Lady Macbeth evokes it (I v 54) and then finds herself its prisoner, endlessly sleepwalking through the thick night of a darkened mind. Macbeth succumbs to its embrace so completely that, in the end, even a "night-shriek" cannot stir him.

Or again, consider blood. "What bloody man is that?" are the play's first words, following the first weyard sisters' scene. Like the night, blood is both ordinary and special. It sticks like real blood: "His secret murders sticking on his hands," says Angus of Macbeth (V ii 20). It smells as real blood smells: "Here's the smell of the blood still," says Lady Macbeth (V i 44), hopelessly washing. Yet it finally covers everything Macbeth has touched, in ways both qualitative and quantitative, that real blood could not. The sleeping grooms are "all badged" (II iii 112) with it, their daggers "Unmannerly breeched with gore" (II iii 127). Duncan's silver skin is "laced" with it (II iii 123), Banquo's murderer has it on his face (III iv 13), Banquo's hair is "boltered" with it (IV i 134), and Macbeth's feet are soaked in it (III iv 162-64). Perhaps the two most bloodcurdling lines in the play, when expressively spoken, are Macbeth's lines after the ghost of Banquo is gone: "It will have blood, they say:/ Blood will have blood" (III iv 146-47) and Lady Macbeth's moaning cry as she washes and washes: "Yet who would have thought the old man to have had so much blood in him?" (V i 34-5).

Macbeth's style of speech in the play has something of this same double character. The startling thing about much of it is its inwardness, as if it were spoken not with the voice at all, but somewhere deep in the arteries and veins, communing with remote strange powers.

    . . . Light thickens,
And the crow makes wing to th' rooky wood.

Good things of day begin to droop and drowse,
Whiles night's black agents to their preys do rouse.
(III ii 57-60)

Between the two battles that open and close the play, Macbeth's language seems frequently to lean away from the historical world of Scotland toward the registering of such experience as rises, timeless and spaceless, both from within his mind and beyond it. Thence come thronging those images that "unfix my hair" (I iii 147), the presences that will "blow the horrid deed in every eye" (I vii 24), the voices that cry "Sleep no more!" (II ii 43), the ghost that returns from the dead to mock him for what he has failed to achieve, and the apparitions that are called with great effort from some nether (but also inner) world only to offer him the very counsels that he most wants to hear.

These continuous blurrings of the "real" with the "unreal," intrusions of what is past and supposedly finished into the present (Banquo's ghost, III iv) and even into the theoretically still formless future (Banquo's descendants, IV i), provide an appropriate sort of environment for Macbeth and his wife. Lady Macbeth is easily "transported," we learn from her first words to her husband, "beyond/This ignorant present" to feel "The future in the instant" (I v 61-63). In a similar way, Macbeth's imagination leaps constantly from what is now to what is to come, from the weyard sisters' prophecy to Duncan's murder, from being "thus" to being "safely thus" (III i 54), from the menace of Banquo to the menace of Macduff, and from a today that is known to an unknown "To-morrow, and to-morrow, and to-morrow" (V v 19). Shakespeare vividly records in these ways the restlessness of the Macbeths' ambition and at the same time the problem that ambition, like every other natural urge to self-realization, poses for human beings and their relationships to each other.

viii

To understand this problem in the dramatic and poetic terms Shakespeare gives it, we must look now at two striking features of the play that have not so far been mentioned. One is feasting. Macbeth withdraws from the supper he has laid for Duncan to weigh the arguments for killing him (I vii). The entertainment, which he has himself ordered, marks his adherence to the community of mutual service that we find implied in the scene at Duncan's court (I iv). Here is a society, we realize, that depends on thane cherishing king—"The service and the loyalty I owe," Macbeth tells Duncan, "In doing it pays itself" (I iv 25-26)—and on king cherishing thane: "I have begun to plant thee," Duncan assures Macbeth, "and will labor/ To make thee full of growing" (I iv 33-34). When Macbeth withdraws, therefore, we see him retreating from the shared community of the supper that he has provided for Duncan and the other thanes into the isolation that his intended crime against that community implies. Once he has withdrawn and his withdrawal is sealed by murder, he can never rejoin the community he has ruptured. This he discovers at the feast in III iv, when the ghost of Banquo preempts his place. The only community left him after this is the community of dark powers we see him appealing to in IV i, where the weyard sisters dance about a hell-broth (also a feast?) of dislocated fragments. After III iv, we never see Macbeth in the company of more than one or two other persons, usually servants, and in the last act his forces ebb inexorably away till there is only himself. Similarly, and with similar implications, after III iv we never see Macbeth and his wife together. Instead of being united by the crime, they are increasingly separated by it, she gradually lost in the inner hell that she finds so "murky" in the sleepwalking scene, he always busier in the outer hell that he has made Scotland into.

The other striking feature is children. Four children have roles in the play: Donalbain, Malcolm, Fleance, and the son of Macduff. Two children are among the apparitions raised by the weyard sisters in IV i: "a bloody child" and "a child crowned, with a tree in his hand." Allusions to children occur often. We hear, for instance, of the child or children Lady Macbeth must have sometime had (I vii 59), of the son Macbeth wishes he had now to succeed him (III i 67-70), and of pity, who comes "like a naked new-born babe/Striding the blast" to trumpet forth Macbeth's murderous act till "tears shall drown the wind" (I vii 21-25). Plainly, in some measure, all these "children" relate to what the play is telling us about time. Macbeth, in his Scottish world (though not in his demonic one), belongs like the rest of us to a world of time: he has been Glamis, he is Cawdor, and he shall be (so the weyard sisters predict) "King hereafter" (I iii 52). The crux, of course, is *hereafter*. Macbeth and his wife seek to make hereafter now, to wrench the future into the present by main force, to master time destructively. But this option, the play seems to be saying, is always disastrous for human beings. The only way human beings can fruitfully master time is Banquo's way, letting it grow and unfold from the present as the Stuart line of kings is to grow and unfold from Fleance. The more Macbeth seeks to control the future, the more there is of it to counter and defeat him (Fleance, Donalbain, Malcolm, the bloody child, the crowned child) and the more he is himself cut off from its creative unfolding processes —having *had* children we are told, but having now only a "fruitless" crown, a "barren" scepter. "No son of mine succeeding" (III i 67-70).

ix

Toward the play's end, Malcolm and his soldiers move in on Dunsinane with their "leavy screens" (V vi 2), and very soon after this Macduff, the man who "was from his mother's womb/ Untimely ripped," meets Macbeth (V viii), slays him, then reappears with his head fixed on a pike. What did Shakespeare intend us to make of this? All that can be said for certain is that the situation on stage in these scenes has some sort of allusive relation to the three apparitions that were summoned at Macbeth's wish by the weyard sisters. The first was an armed head—matched here at the play's end, apparently, by Macbeth's armed head on a pike. The second was a bloody child, who told him that none of woman born could harm him. This child is evidently to be associated with Macduff. The third apparition was a crowned child holding a tree—an allusion, we may suppose, to Malcolm, child of Duncan, who is soon to be crowned King, who is part of the future that Macbeth has tried in vain to control, and who now with his men, holding the green branches of Birnam Wood, seems calculated to remind us of the way in which Nature, green, fertile, "full of growing," moves inexorably to "overgrow" a man who has more and more identified himself with death and all such destructive uses of power as the armed head suggests. If these speculations are at all well founded, what takes place in the final scenes is that a kind of Living Death, a figure who has alienated himself from all the growing processes, goes out to war encased in an armor that he believes to be invulnerable on the ground that nothing in the scheme of nature, nothing born of woman, can conquer Death. But he is wrong. Death can always be conquered by the bloody child, who, being ripped from the womb as his mother lay dying, is indicative of the life that in Nature's scheme of things (like the green leaves in Birnam Wood) is always being reborn from death.

x

To leave the play on this abstract and allegorical plane, however, is to do it wrong. What comes home most sharply to us as we watch these last scenes performed is the twistings and turnings of a ruined but fascinating human being, a human being capable of profound even if disbalanced insights, probing the boundaries of our common nature ever more deeply in frantically changing accesses of arrogance and despair, defiance and cowardice, lethargy and exhilaration, folly and wisdom. For background to this, we have the succession of abrupt changes from place to place, group to group, and speaker to speaker that marks scenes ii to viii in Act V, an unsettling discontinuity which does much to dramatize our sense of a kingdom coming apart at the seams. In the background, too, we hear the gradually swelling underbeat of the allied drums, called for by the stage directions in V ii, iv, vi, and viii, and audible elsewhere if the director desires. This gives a sensory dimension to the increasing prosperity of Malcolm's cause, and can be made particularly dramatic and significant in V v. Here, following the scene's opening, we hear Macbeth's drums for the only time in the play. Then comes the famous soliloquy, where he assures us that life is an empty fraud, a "tale told by an idiot." If, at the close of this, when the door to Dunsinane opens to admit the messenger bearing the news of Birnam Wood, we hear again in the distance the steady beat of the allied drums signifying the existence of a very different point of view about the value of life, the impact is electric.

Perhaps the most telling sensory effect of all in these final scenes is the use of trumpets. We hear them first on the appearance of Macduff (V vi 11-12), whose command may remind us of Macbeth's earlier prognostication about "heaven's

cherubin" riding the winds and blowing the fame—or infamy—
of the murder of Duncan through the whole world:

> Make all our trumpets speak, give them all breath,
> Those clamorous harbingers of blood and death.

We then hear their alarums with the next entry of Macduff, who
is now searching for Macbeth, and again with the exit of Malcolm; alarums once more when Macduff and Macbeth begin to
fight and when they go fighting off stage; and finally, three
massed flourishes of trumpets, one as Malcolm enters after the
sounding of retreat (V viii 40), a second as Macduff and the
other thanes hail Malcolm king (V viii 71), and a third as all
go out, Macbeth's head waving somberly on Macduff's spear.
The former age has been wiped away and the new age inaugurated, fittingly, to the sound of the trumpets of Judgment.

All this, we understand, is as it must be. Alike as ruler
and man, Macbeth has been tried and found wanting. Yet we
realize, as we hear Malcolm speak of "this dead butcher and
his fiend-like queen" (V viii 81)—and we realize it all the more
because of these last scenes, in which a great man goes down
fighting, bayed around by enemies external and internal, natural
and even supernatural, committed to the Father of Lies but
taking the consequences like a man—how much there is that
Judgment does not know, and how much there is that, through
Shakespeare's genius, we do.

<hr/>

A Note on the Elizabethan Theater

Most present-day productions of Elizabethan plays use
sets designed to provide a single flexible and suggestive background against which their multiple scenes can flow easily one
into the next. Elizabethan plays have to be staged that way if
they are not to be distorted, because that is the way they are
built. Though the modern playwright is limited by the nature
of his theater to as few changes of locale as possible, his Elizabethan counterpart was encouraged by *his* theater to range the

whole world of space and time, because his theater was in fact an image of the world. Shakespeare's own theater was even called the world—i.e. the "Globe."

In today's theaters, for the most part, audience and play are emphatically separate. They are separated physically by the architecture of the theater, which has a drop-curtain, footlights, often an orchestra pit, and always a proscenium arch (the arch covered by the curtain), on one side of which the audience sits hushed in almost total darkness, while on the other side the persons of the play move and talk in spots, or floods, of blazing light.

This physical separation of audience from play is expressive of the figurative gulf which, in our theater, also divides them. For the illusion that the modern theater imposes is that the audience is "not really" present, but is eavesdropping, and that the people it looks in on are "really" men and women going about real business in a real room from which one wall has been removed.

What this means for those on the bright side of the footlights is that everything must be made as completely "present" as actors, scene-painters, and stage-carpenters can manage; it is not enough to suggest reality, it must be simulated. The implication for those on the dark side of the footlights is that they must become as "unpresent" as they can—in other words detached, silent, and passive, like the eavesdroppers they are. Actually, neither of these extremes is ever reached in our theater, or even closely approached, but the tendency of enhanced realism on one side of the curtain to generate passivity on the other has spurred many modern playwrights to search for ways of recapturing the cooperative relation between audience and play that Shakespeare's theater had.

Physically the Globe was a wooden building shaped probably like a polygon outside and circular inside, some thirty or forty feet high, with three tiers of roofed galleries, one on top of the other straight up, opera-house style, around the entire interior. The center of the enclosure (the "pit"), some fifty or so feet in diameter, was unroofed, and into it jutted the raised rectangular stage, fully half the way across the pit and almost forty feet wide. Above part of the stage, as a cover, supported on pillars, was a sloping roof, called the "Heavens," the ceiling of which

THE GLOBE PLAYHOUSE, 1599–1613

A Conjectural Reconstruction

Key

AA Main entrance
B The Yard
CC Entrances to lowest gallery
D Entrances to staircase and upper galleries
E Corridor serving the different sections of the middle gallery
F Middle gallery ("Twopenny Rooms")
G "Gentlemen's Rooms" or "Lords' Rooms"
H The stage
J The hanging being put up around the stage
K The "Hell" under the stage
L The stage trap, leading down to the "Hell"
MM Stage doors
N Curtained "place behind the stage"
O Gallery above the stage, used as required—sometimes by musicians, sometimes by spectators, and often as part of the play
P Backstage area (the tiring-house)
Q Tiring-house door
R Dressing rooms
S Wardrobe and storage
T The hut housing the machine for lowering enthroned gods, etc., to the stage
U The "Heavens"
W Hoisting the playhouse flag

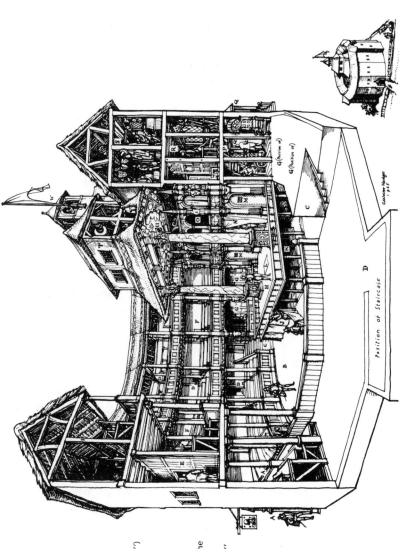

was brightly painted with stars and other astronomical figures. Below the stage, reached by trap doors, was "Hell." At the rear wall, doors on either side gave access between the stage and the dressing rooms. Toward the rear of the stage there was an "inner" playing area, probably a sort of alcove (but sometimes misleadingly called the "inner stage"), which could be left opened or curtained. Directly above this was an "upper" playing area (the "upper stage"), which probably took the form of a balcony. Above this was another, smaller balcony for the musicians; for the use of music, in tragedy as well as comedy, was one of the conventions of Elizabethan plays.

What scenery there was in theaters like the Globe took chiefly the form of simple props. There was no artificial lighting of any kind in the theater, which meant that performances were always given by daylight—in the afternoon. The interior of the building was handsomely decorated, and the dress of the actors (males only—boys played the female roles) expensive and resplendent, although there was little concern for what we would call authentic period costuming.

The important thing to bear in mind about the Elizabethan theater is that the stage physically dominated the open area and that the audience literally enveloped the actors and the action. As many as two thousand people might be present. Many stood shoulder to shoulder in the pit, surrounding the chest-high open platform on three sides. Behind them in the tiered galleries, at no place more than forty or fifty feet from the stage, sat hundreds of others on benches. In these circumstances, it was easy for the viewers' sense of involvement in the play, and the actors' sense of involvement with the audience before and behind them, to become more intense than in our theater.

The playwright who writes for such a theater as this cannot shape his play as if the audience were not "there": it is irremovably there, every member of it visible to every other in the broad light coming from the open roof. So he necessarily acknowledges its presence, engages its imagination. He feels free, for example, to give his characters "asides"—speeches spoken wholly or mainly for the benefit of the audience, and which those on stage are not supposed to hear. He also gives his characters "soliloquies"—longer speeches by means of which the leading characters may open heart and mind directly to the audience. Further, since his stage is a bare platform without scenery, he calls repeatedly on the imagination of the audience to flesh out the suggestions of hour, place, weather, or mood that he can only communicate to them through the play's own words.

The dramatist who writes for the theater we have been describing has unparalleled opportunities to make the theater audience do duty as an extension, an overflow, an amplification of the very limited stage-audiences which a small company of actors can muster. When, for instance, Shakespeare's Antony addresses the Roman mob in *Julius Caesar*, in a theater where we of the audience surround him on three sides, the realization comes on us increasingly as he speaks that it is we who fill out that tiny group of listeners onstage into the formidable mob he *seems* to harangue; and when King Harry in *Henry V* exhorts his soldiers—"You noblest English"—to battle bravely against the French, we realize (as Shakespeare's own audiences must have done, and in their case with a sharp quickening of the pulse) that it is *we* who are being addressed: *we* are those "noblest English" who are being implored never to yield.

Interactions like these between play and audience are not impossible in the modern theater, but they were a good deal easier to effect in Shakespeare's. Partly, as we have noticed, because of the close physical proximity of audience to player. Partly, as we have also noticed, because the audience's imagination was implicated in the play by the very austerity of a stage without scenery. And partly because the Elizabethan theater's inheritance from the medieval theater (where the stories acted out were primarily Bible stories and therefore "true" in one sense while remaining "stories" in another sense) encouraged an easy traffic back and forth between what was "real" and what was "play."

As has been mentioned, over part of the stage stretched a ceiling called the "Heavens," and under the stage, reached by trap doors through which witches and other apparitions might rise, lay an area called "Hell." And in front of the theater, in the case of Shakespeare's Globe (if we may believe a plausible tradition), was inscribed the legend: *Totus mundus agit histrionem*—"Everybody is an actor"; or, as Shakespeare himself paraphrased it in *As You Like It,* "All the world's a stage, and all the men and women merely players." Thus the individual actor whom the audience saw on the stage playing Julius Caesar or Hamlet or Macbeth was capable of being translated, at any moment, by the very symbolism of that stage, into an image of Every Man working out his human destiny (as the men and women watching him would also have to work out theirs) between the powers of Hell and Heaven.

It is because the characters of Shakespeare were created for a theater like this that they take special hold of us. They have the intensity that comes from believing that the world is a stage, where we are given only our little hour to work out eternal salvation or damnation: and they have the grandeur that comes from believing that the stage is a world, which reaches out past the actors to the theater audience, past them to the audience we call history, past this to the cosmic audience of land, sea, air, moon, sun, and stars (which Elizabethan heroes do not hesitate to address), and so at last to the audience Hamlet turns to when the appearance of the Ghost makes it unmistakable that there are more things in heaven and earth than are dreamed of in human philosophies: "Angels and ministers of grace defend us!"

Textual Note

Although Shakespeare had no connection with their actual publication, eighteen of his thirty-seven plays were published in various quarto editions before his death in 1616. Not until 1623 were all but one of the plays usually credited to him published in a single volume, now called the First Folio. (A folio is a book made up of sheets folded in half, creating four individual pages per sheet; a quarto is one made up of sheets folded in half and in half again, producing eight pages per sheet.) The First Folio was compiled by two of Shakespeare's actor-colleagues who drew upon the best previous quarto editions of single plays, where available, and on fairly reliable unpublished manuscripts and theater promptbooks. For whatever reason, they omitted from their collection two plays which most scholars today attribute wholly or in part to Shakespeare (*Pericles, Prince of Tyre* and *The Two Noble Kinsmen*) and one play (*Sir Thomas More*) in which it is believed he had a hand.

The policy of these editions of the plays is to use the earliest sound version of each play—either the Folio text or (if one exists) a good quarto text with collations from the Folio—and a minimum of emendation. In lineation, we follow a similarly conservative policy. Most modern editors space the line fragments, with which two successive speeches often end and begin, as a single pentameter line. A case can be made for this procedure, but after considerable reflection we have abandoned it, because we believe that in these situations the lineation of the original editions more often than not throws interesting light on speaking emphasis, pause, and rhythm, and also eliminates a possible reading distraction. We have everywhere normalized and modernized the spelling and punctuation of the original texts, printed character names in full, and added (inconspicuously) act-scene divisions, following the practice of the Globe edition (1864), to which concordances of Shakespeare refer. All matter placed in brackets in the text, including stage directions, is editorial and does not appear in the original version being used.

The line numbering and the act-scene indicators at the top of each page are for convenient reference. The small degree sign (°) indicates a gloss or footnote at the bottom of the page, keyed by line number. The cue phrase is printed in boldface, the gloss or footnote in roman.

The only authoritative text of *Macbeth* is found in the First Folio. The play shows a few signs of interpolation in the later witch scenes and agreement is now pretty general that Hecate had no part in the play as Shakespeare wrote it, and that, accordingly, III v, together with IV i 39-43, and possibly 136-43, which clash in tone with the atmosphere that surrounds the witches elsewhere, are insertions by another hand. Arguments that the play has been heavily revised and cut have met with less acceptance, since nothing material seems to be missing from it in its present form. There *may* have been extensive revision and cutting or there may have been only the interpolations above mentioned—we shall never know.

THE TRAGEDY OF

MACBETH

[Dramatis Personae

DUNCAN, King of Scotland

MALCOLM ⎫
DONALBAIN ⎭ his sons

MACBETH ⎫
BANQUO ⎪
MACDUFF ⎪
LENNOX ⎪
ROSS ⎬ noblemen of Scotland
MENTEITH ⎪
ANGUS ⎪
CAITHNESS ⎭

FLEANCE, son to Banquo

SIWARD, Earl of Northumberland

YOUNG SIWARD, his son

SEYTON, an officer attending on Macbeth

BOY, son to Macduff

A CAPTAIN

AN ENGLISH DOCTOR

A SCOTTISH DOCTOR

A PORTER

AN OLD MAN

THREE MURDERERS

LADY MACBETH

LADY MACDUFF

A GENTLEWOMAN, attending on Lady Macbeth

THE WEIRD SISTERS

HECATE

THE GHOST OF BANQUO

APPARITIONS

LORDS, OFFICERS, SOLDIERS, MESSENGERS, ATTENDANTS

Scene: Scotland and England]

THE TRAGEDY OF

MACBETH

[handwritten: opening line: question - creates sense of doubt witch's have already met.]

Thunder and lightning. Enter three Witches.   I i

1. WITCH.   When shall we three meet again?
   In thunder, lightning, or in rain?   *[handwritten: announce fact, don't create it]*
2. WITCH.   When the hurlyburly's done,   *[handwritten: confusion]*
   When the battle's lost and won. *[handwritten: — paradox]*
3. WITCH.   That will be ere the set of sun.   5

1. WITCH.   Where the place? *[handwritten: — question]*

2. WITCH.   Upon the heath.

3. WITCH.   There to meet with Macbeth.

1. WITCH.   I come, Graymalkin!

2. WITCH.   Paddock° calls.   10

3. WITCH.   Anon!°

ALL.   Fair is foul, and foul is fair. *[handwritten: — foreshadowing in a paradox]*
   Hover through the fog and filthy air.   *Exeunt.*

I i 9-10 **Graymalkin, Paddock** "familiar spirits," or companion demons, of the witches, here conceived of as possessing the bodies of a gray cat and a toad
11 Anon   i.e. I come at once
10-13 Paddock . . . air the Folio assigns these lines to "All," but in fact in 10-11 the second and third witches seem to be answering individually to their familiar spirits as the first witch does in 9

Alarum within.° Enter King [Duncan], Malcolm, Donalbain,   I ii
Lennox, with Attendants, meeting a bleeding Captain.
                  becomes a motif
KING.   What bloody man is that? He can report,
     As seemeth by his plight, of the revolt

things aren't
the way they The newest state.°
seem

MALCOLM.   This is the sergeant°
     Who like a good and hardy soldier fought   5
     'Gainst my captivity.° Hail, brave friend!
     Say to the King the knowledge of the broil°
     As thou didst leave it.

CAPTAIN.   Doubtful it stood,
     As two spent swimmers that do cling together   10
     And choke their art. The merciless Macdonwald
     (Worthy to be a rebel, for to that°
     The multiplying villainies° of nature
     Do swarm upon him) from the Western Isles°
     Of° kerns° and gallowglasses° is supplied;   15
     And Fortune, on his damnèd quarrel smiling,
     Showed like a rebel's whore.° But all's too weak:
     For brave Macbeth (well he deserves that name),
     Disdaining Fortune, with his brandished steel,
     Which smoked° with bloody execution,°   20
     Like valor's minion° carved out his passage
     Till he faced the slave;
     Which° ne'er shook hands° nor bade farewell to him
     Till he unseamed him from the nave to th' chops°
     And fixed his head upon our battlements.   25

KING.   O valiant cousin!° worthy gentleman!

I ii s.d. Alarum within trumpet call off-stage
2-3 of . . . state i.e. the current progress of the rebel invasion
4 sergeant (3 syllables) field officer (not a rank: as the s.d. indicates, this sergeant is a captain)
6 my captivity my being captured
7 broil quarrel
12 to that to that end
13 multiplying villainies all the vices (here conceived of as vermin) possible to human nature
14 Western Isles Hebrides (including Ireland?)
15 Of with
15 kerns Irish foot soldiers lightly armed

15 gallowglasses Irish cavalry armed with axes
17 Showed . . . whore i.e. deceived him by bringing success at first
20 smoked steamed (with the hot blood)
20 execution ("ion" is disyllabic here and often elsewhere in the play, e.g. 21 "minion", 27 "reflection", and I v 35 "preparation")
21 minion favorite
23 Which i.e. Macdonwald
23 ne'er shook hands was not allowed to leave
24 nave . . . chops navel to the jaws
26 cousin (this normally means any kinsman, but Shakespeare's Macbeth is in fact first cousin to Duncan)

CAPTAIN.   As whence the sun 'gins his reflection°
        Shipwracking storms and direful thunders [break],°
        So far that spring whence comfort seemed to come
        Discomfort swells. Mark, King of Scotland, mark.   30
        No sooner justice had, with valor armed,
        Compelled these skipping kerns to trust their heels
        But the Norweyan lord,° surveying vantage,°
        With furbished° arms and new supplies of men,
        Began a fresh assault.°   35

KING.   Dismayed not this our captains, Macbeth and Banquo?

CAPTAIN.   Yes, as sparrows eagles,
        Or the hare the lion.
        If I say sooth,° I must report they were
        As cannons overcharged with double cracks,°   40
        So they doubly redoubled strokes upon the foe.
        Except° they meant to bathe in reeking wounds,
        Or memorize another Golgotha,°
        I cannot tell—but I am faint,
        My gashes cry for help.   45

KING.   So well thy words become thee as thy wounds,
        They smack of honor both. Go get him surgeons.
                                [Exit Captain, attended.]

                        Enter Ross and Angus.

        Who comes here?

MALCOLM.   The worthy Thane° of Ross.

LENNOX.   What a haste looks through his eyes!   50
        So should he look that seems to° speak things strange.

ROSS.   God save the king!

KING.   Whence cam'st thou, worthy thane?

---

27 **reflection** shining
28 **break** not in First Folio; supplied from
"breaking" in Second Folio
33 **Norweyan lord** Sveno, king of Norway
33 **surveying vantage** seeing an advantage
34 **furbished** freed of rust, i.e. readied
again for use
27-35 **As whence . . . assault** i.e. as bad
things ("storms") may come from the same
source as good (the "sun") so the Nor-
wegian attack struck us at the moment of
victory over Macdonwald

39 **sooth** truth
40 **double cracks** (1) double charges (?)
(2) doubled noise (?)
42 **Except** unless
43 **memorize . . . Golgotha** make this
battlefield   as   memorable   as   Golgotha
("place of the dead," the place where
Jesus was crucified)
49 **Thane** (a Scottish title of nobility)
51 **seems to** seems about to

Ross.   From Fife, great king,
    Where the Norweyan banners flout° the sky   55
    And fan our people cold.
    Norway° himself, with terrible numbers,— *lots of men*
    Assisted by that most disloyal traitor ~~Macdonwald~~
    The Thane of Cawdor, began a dismal° conflict, *God of war*
    Till that Bellona's bridegroom,° lapped in proof,° 60
    Confronted him with self-comparisons,°
    Point against point, rebellious arm 'gainst arm,
    Curbing his lavish° spirit: and to conclude,
    The victory fell on us.

KING.   Great happiness!   65

Ross.   That° now Sweno, the Norways' king,
    Craves composition;°
    Nor would we deign him burial of his men
    Till he disbursèd, at Saint Colme's Inch,°
    Ten thousand dollars° to our general use.   70

KING.   No more that Thane of Cawdor shall deceive
    Our bosom interest.° Go pronounce his present° death *Heroic*
    And with his former title greet Macbeth.   *Couplet*

Ross.   I'll see it done.

KING.   What he hath lost noble Macbeth hath won. *Exeunt.* 75

〜◦◉◦〜✕〜◦◉◦〜

Thunder. Enter the three Witches.   *I iii*

1. WITCH.   Where has thou been, sister?

2. WITCH.   Killing swine.°

---

55 **flout** insult
57 **Norway** i.e. the King of Norway
59 **dismal** ill-omened
60 **Bellona's bridegroom** i.e. Macbeth (as if taken for husband by the goddess of war)
60 **lapped in proof** wrapped in proven armor
61 **self-comparisons** powers equal to his own
63 **lavish** wild
66 **That** with the result that

67 **composition** peace terms
69 **Saint . . . Inch** Inchcolm, an island in the Firth of Forth
70 **dollars** Spanish ("dolares") and German ("Thalers") coins, first coined ca. 1518
72 **Our . . . interest** i.e. that closest to our (royal plural) heart
72 **present** immediate
I iii 2 **Killing swine** i.e. destroying the one possession of most of the rural poor

3. WITCH.   Sister, where thou?

1. WITCH.   A sailor's wife had chestnuts in her lap
    And mounched and mounched and mounched.   5
    "Give me," quoth I.
    "Aroint thee,° witch!" the rump-fed ronyon° cries.
    Her husband's to Aleppo gone, master o' th' Tiger:°
    But in a sieve° I'll thither sail   ~*ship*
    And, like a rat without a tail,°   10
    I'll do, I'll do, and I'll do.

2. WITCH.   I'll give thee a wind.°

1. WITCH.   Th' art kind.

3. WITCH.   And I another.

1. WITCH.   I myself have all the other,°   15
    And the very ports they° blow,
    All the quarters that they know
    I' th' shipman's card.°
    I'll drain him dry as hay.°
    Sleep shall neither night nor day   20
    Hang upon his penthouse lid.°
    He shall live a man forbid.°
    Weary sev'nights, nine times nine,
    Shall he dwindle, peak,° and pine.
    Though his bark cannot be lost,   25
    Yet it shall be tempest-tost.°
    Look what I have.

2. WITCH.   Show me, show me.

1. WITCH.   Here I have a pilot's thumb,°
    Wracked as homeward he did come.   *Drum within.* 30

---

7 **Aroint thee** begone
7 **rump-fed ronyon** fat-rumped scabby creature
8 **Tiger** (a common name for ships in Shakespeare's day)
9 **sieve** (thought to be the usual craft for sea-going witches)
10 **like . . . tail** i.e. taking the shape of a rat, but imperfect, as the devil's creatures must be
12 **I'll . . . wind** (witches were believed to have dominion of the winds)
15 **other** i.e. other winds
16 **they** i.e. to which they
18 **card** compass

19 **I'll . . . hay** I'll keep him at sea, unable to make port, till all his water is gone and he is as dry as hay
21 **penthouse lid** eyelid (seen as a lean-to)
22 **forbid** accursed
24 **peak** waste away
25-26 **Though . . . tempest-tost** (evidently the *Tiger* is destined for a safe return; the witch can only make the voyage miserable and long)
29 **thumb** (such fragments were used in black magic as charms to facilitate or obstruct specific events—here to obstruct the return of the *Tiger*—see IV i 1-38)

3. WITCH.   A drum, a drum!
    Macbeth doth come.

ALL.   The weyard° sisters, hand in hand,
    Posters° of the sea and land,
    Thus do go about, about,   35
    Thrice to thine, and thrice to mine,
    And thrice again, to make up nine.°
    Peace! The charm's wound up.°

        Enter Macbeth and Banquo.

MACBETH.   So foul and fair a day I have not seen.

BANQUO.   How far is't called to Forres?° What are these,   40
    So withered and so wild in their attire
    That look not like th' inhabitants o' th' earth
    And yet are on't? Live you, or are you aught
    That man may question?° You seem to understand me,
    By each at once her choppy° finger laying   45
    Upon her skinny lips. You should be women,
    And yet your beards° forbid me to interpret
    That you are so.

MACBETH.   Speak, if you can. What are you?

1. WITCH.   All hail, Macbeth! Hail to thee, Thane of Glamis!   50

2. WITCH.   All hail, Macbeth! Hail to thee, Thane of Cawdor!

3. WITCH.   All hail, Macbeth, that shalt be King hereafter!

BANQUO.   Good sir, why do you start and seem to fear
    Things that do sound so fair? I' th' name of truth,
    Are ye fantastical,° or that indeed   55
    Which outwardly ye show? My noble partner
    You greet with present grace and great prediction
    Of noble having and of royal hope,°
    That he seems rapt withal.° To me you speak not.

---

33 weyard fate-serving (the Folio varies
between this spelling and "weyward" but
never has "weird," which in its modern
connotations badly misrepresents the witches;
this edition has "weyard" throughout)
34 Posters swift travelers
36-37 Thrice . . . nine three and nine are
"magic" numbers; here the witches, in their
dance, may be making bows and mows
(faces) at their invisible "familiars": see
note I i 9-10
38 wound up i.e. ready to unwind to the
desired result

40 Forres location of Duncan's palace
44 question lawfully address
45 choppy chapped
47 beards a beard was often taken to be
a sign that a woman was a witch
55 fantastical imaginary
57-58 present . . . hope i.e. Glamis
(which he is), Cawdor (which he has been
made, though he does not know it yet), and
king
59 rapt withal entranced by it

If you can look into the seeds of time   60
And say which grain will grow and which will not,
Speak then to me, who neither beg nor fear
Your favors nor your hate.

1. WITCH.   Hail!

2. WITCH.   Hail!   65

3. WITCH.   Hail!

1. WITCH.   Lesser than Macbeth, and greater.°

2. WITCH.   Not so happy, yet much happier.

3. WITCH.   Thou shalt get° kings, though thou be none.
So all hail, Macbeth and Banquo!   70

1. WITCH.   Banquo and Macbeth, all hail!

MACBETH.   Stay, you imperfect° speakers, tell me more:
By Sinel's° death I know I am Thane of Glamis,
But how of Cawdor? The Thane of Cawdor lives,
A prosperous gentleman; and to be King   75
Stands not within the prospect° of belief,
No more than to be Cawdor. Say from whence
You owe° this strange intelligence,° or why
Upon this blasted heath you stop our way
With such prophetic greeting.   80
Speak, I charge you.   *Witches vanish.*

BANQUO.   The earth hath bubbles as the water has,
And these are of them. Whither are they vanished?

MACBETH.   Into the air, and what seemed corporal°
Melted as breath into the wind.   85
Would they had stayed.

BANQUO.   Were such things here as we do speak about?
Or have we eaten on the insane° root
That takes the reason prisoner?

MACBETH.   Your children shall be kings.   90

---

67 Lesser . . . greater i.e. less than Macbeth in fortune but a greater man; not so felicitous in the positions you will occupy, but for that very reason much happier in mind
69 get beget
72 imperfect i.e. unfinished (they have not told him all he wants to know)

73 Sinel (his father)
76 prospect outlook
78 owe own
78 intelligence information
84 corporal corporeal
88 insane i.e. madness-producing (such as hemlock, for example, was supposed to be)

BANQUO.   You shall be King.

MACBETH.   And Thane of Cawdor too. Went it not so?

BANQUO.   To th' selfsame tune and words. Who's here?

Enter Ross and Angus.

ROSS.   The King hath happily received, Macbeth,
    The news of thy success; and when he reads°   95
    Thy personal venture in the rebels' fight,
    His wonders and his praises do contend
    Which should be thine or his.° Silenced with that,°
    In viewing o'er the rest o' th' selfsame day,
    He finds thee in the stout Norweyan ranks,   100
    Nothing° afeard of what thyself didst make,
    Strange images of death.° As thick as hail°
    Came post with post,° and every one did bear
    Thy praises in his kingdom's great defense
    And poured them down before him.   105

ANGUS.   We are sent
    To give thee from our royal master thanks;
    Only to herald thee into his sight,
    Not pay thee.

ROSS.   And for an earnest° of a greater honor,   110
    He bade me, from him, call thee Thane of Cawdor;
    In which addition,° hail, most worthy Thane,
    For it is thine.

BANQUO.   What, can the devil° speak true?

MACBETH.   The Thane of Cawdor lives.   115
    Why do you dress me in borrowed robes?

---

95 reads considers
97-98 His wonders . . . or his i.e. he longs
to speak your praises, which would make
them "thine," but is struck dumb with ad-
miration, which keeps them unuttered (i.e.
"his")
98 that the conflict just mentioned
101 Nothing not at all
102 Strange . . . death i.e. death in all the
grotesque forms in which it shows itself in
the postures and agonies of the dead and
dying
102 As . . . hail (the Folio has "As . . .
tale," which some editors retain, interpreting

it to mean "as fast as can be tallied, i.e.
counted"; but the phrase is unprecedented
in Shakespeare [as is also "tale" in this
sense] and the interpretation seems strained;
it is true, on the other hand, that Shakespeare nowhere else spells "hail" as "hale")
103 post with post messenger after messenger
110 earnest i.e. down payment on a larger
debt
112 addition i.e. title
114 devil (often one syllable, de'il, as
here)

ANGUS.   Who° was the Thane lives yet,
          But under heavy judgment bears that life
          Which he deserves to lose.
          Whether he was combined° with those of Norway,   120
          Or did line the rebel° with hidden help
          And vantage,° or that with both he labored
          In his country's wrack,° I know not;
          But treasons capital,° confessed and proved,
          Have overthrown him.   125

MACBETH.   [*aside*] Glamis, and Thane of Cawdor—
          The greatest is behind!° [*to Ross and Angus*] Thanks for
               your pains.
          [*Aside to Banquo*] Do you not hope your children shall be
               kings,
          When those that gave the Thane of Cawdor to me
          Promised no less to them?   130

BANQUO.   [*to Macbeth*] That, trusted home,°
          Might yet enkindle you unto° the crown,
          Besides the Thane of Cawdor. But 'tis strange:°
          And oftentimes, to win us to our harm,
          The instruments of darkness tell us truths,   135
          Win us with honest trifles, to betray's
          In deepest consequence.°—
          Cousins,° a word, I pray you.

MACBETH.   [*aside*] Two truths are told,
          As happy prologues to the swelling° act°   140
          Of the imperial theme.—I thank you, gentlemen.—
          [*Aside*] This supernatural soliciting°
          Cannot be ill, cannot be good.
          If ill, why hath it given me earnest° of success,

---

117 **Who** i.e. the man who
120 **combined** leagued
121 **line . . . rebel** support Macdonwald
122 **vantage** advantage
123 **wrack** wreck, i.e. ruin
124 **capital** punishable by death
127 **is behind** remains to come
131 **home** i.e. all the way
132 **unto** to hope for
133 **strange** (referring to the speedy fulfillment of the prophecy)
137 **In . . . consequence** (1) in matters of vital significance (?) (2) when what we

expect to follow or be consequent upon the trifle fails to occur (?)
138 **Cousins** kinsmen
140 **swelling** (1) full of pomp, stately (2) coming to fruition
140 **act** (1) drama (2) deed (in ''act'' Macbeth seems to contemplate his rise to the throne in both spectator terms, as something destined to take place, and participating terms, as something that is to be done)
142 **soliciting** incitement
144 **earnest** see note 110

Commencing in a truth? I am Thane of Cawdor.   145
If good, why do I yield to° that suggestion
Whose horrid image° doth unfix my hair°
And make my seated° heart knock at my ribs
Against the use of nature?° Present fears
Are less than horrible imaginings.°   150
My thought, whose murder yet is but fantastical,°
Shakes so my single state of man°
That function is smothered in surmise
And nothing is but what is not.°

BANQUO.   Look how our partner's rapt.°   155

MACBETH.   [*aside*] If chance will have me King,
Why chance may crown me
Without my stir.°

BANQUO.   New honors come upon him,
Like our strange° garments, cleave not to their mould°   160
But with the aid of use.

MACBETH.   [*aside*] Come what come may,
Time and the hour runs through the roughest day.°

BANQUO.   Worthy Macbeth, we stay upon your leisure.°

MACBETH.   Give me your favor.°   165
My dull brain was wrought° with things forgotten.
Kind gentlemen, your pains are regist'red
Where every day I turn the leaf
To read them.°
Let us toward the King. [*aside to Banquo*] Think upon   170

---

146 **yield to** allow to enter my mind
147 **horrid image** (of Duncan's murder)
147 **unfix my hair** make my hair rise
148 **seated** fixed
149 **the . . . nature** i.e. nature's custom
(Macbeth may mean especially his own nature's custom since he is usually fearless)
149-50 **Present . . . imaginings** terrifying
things one immediately confronts (as in
battle) are less frightening than terrors that
are (a) in the mind ("imaginings") and (b)
still to come
151 **fantastical** imaginary
152 **my . . . man** (1) my normal unity of
being (with a pun on "state" as a nation
or kingdom troubled by insurrection) (2)
my weak human condition
153-54 **function . . . not** i.e. all my normal
functional powers are so swallowed up in
my imagination (of murdering Duncan) that

nothing exists as real for me except what is
not (yet) real, i.e. the murder
155 **rapt** entranced
158 **my stir** any action by me
160 **strange** new
160 **cleave . . . mould** i.e. do not set easily
163 **Time . . . day** i.e. even the roughest
day has an end (the vague image in "time
and the hour" may be that of an hourglass,
with the "day" diminishing like the supply
of sand in the upper half as the glass runs
it through, i.e. through itself)
164 **stay . . . leisure** await your conve-
nience
165 **favor** pardon
166 **wrought** agitated
167-69 **regist'red . . . them** i.e. in his
brain and heart

What hath chanced, and at more time,°
The interim having weighed it,° let us speak
Our free hearts° each to other.

BANQUO.   Very gladly.

MACBETH.   Till then, enough.—   175
Come, friends.   *Exeunt.*

⌒⌒⌒⌒⌒⌒

Flourish.° Enter King [Duncan], Lennox, Malcolm,   I iv
Donalbain, and Attendants.

KING.   Is execution done on Cawdor?
Are not those in commission° yet returned?

MALCOLM.   My liege, they are not yet come back.
But I have spoke with one that saw him die;
Who did report that very frankly he   5
Confessed his treasons, implored your Highness' pardon,
And set forth a deep repentance.
Nothing in his life became him
Like the leaving it. He died
As one that had been studied° in his death   10
To throw away the dearest thing he owed°
As 'twere a careless° trifle.

KING.   There's no art
To find the mind's construction in the face.
He was a gentleman on whom I built   15
An absolute trust.

        Enter Macbeth, Banquo, Ross, and Angus.

O worthiest cousin,
The sin of my ingratitude even now
Was heavy on me. Thou art so far before°

---

171 **time** leisure
172 **weighed it** i.e. given us time to
weigh it
173 **Our . . . hearts** our thoughts freely
I iv s.d. Flourish trumpet fanfare
2 **in commission** commissioned to see
that his sentence is carried out

10 **been studied** taught himself
11 **owed** owned
12 **careless** uncared-for
19 **before** ahead (in deserving)

That swiftest wing of recompense is slow   20
To overtake thee. Would thou hadst less deserved,
That the proportion both of° thanks and payment
Might have been mine! Only I have° left to say,
More is thy due than more than all can pay.

MACBETH.   The service and the loyalty I owe,   25
In doing it pays itself.
Your Highness' part is to receive our duties,
And our duties are to your throne and state
Children and servants, which do but what they should
By doing everything safe toward° your love   30
And honor.

KING.   Welcome hither.
I have begun to plant° thee and will labor
To make thee full of growing.° Noble Banquo,
That hast no less deserved nor must be known   35
No less to have done so, let me enfold thee
And hold thee to my heart.

BANQUO.   There if I grow,
The harvest is your own.

KING.   My plenteous joys,   40
Wanton in fullness, seek to hide themselves
In drops of sorrow.° Sons, kinsmen, thanes,
And you whose places are the nearest,° know
We will establish our estate° upon
Our eldest, Malcolm, whom we name hereafter   45
The Prince of Cumberland;° which honor must
Not unaccompanied° invest him only,
But signs of nobleness, like stars, shall shine

---

22 **the . . . of** matching your merit with
23 **I have** I've (Elizabethan speech often contracts such forms without indicating it in the spelling)
30 **safe toward** i.e. that safeguards
33 **plant** i.e. by making him Thane of Cawdor
34 **full . . . growing** thrive (like a well-tended plant)
41-42 **Wanton . . . sorrow** i.e. his joys are undisciplined (like children, see "hide") because they express themselves in tears
43 **nearest** (to the throne)
44 **establish our estate** settle the succession (the Scottish monarchy was elective

and Macbeth, earlier in the play, could have thought that on Duncan's death he, as the great warrior, might succeed to the throne (I iii 156-58); however, Malcolm's formal installation here as Prince of Cumberland signified that he was recognized by all the Scottish thanes as heir apparent)
46 **Prince of Cumberland** Scottish title corresponding to "Prince of Wales" in England
47 **unaccompanied** i.e. without others also receiving honors

On all deservers. From hence° to Inverness,°
And bind us further to you.   50
MACBETH.   The rest° is labor which is not used for you.
    I'll be myself the harbinger,° and make joyful
    The hearing of my wife with your approach;
    So, humbly take my leave.
KING.   My worthy Cawdor!   *He's thinking distances character* 55
                                                          from mouat
MACBETH.   [*aside*] The Prince of Cumberland—that is a step
    On which I must fall down or else o'erleap,
    For in my way it lies. Stars, hide your fires;
    Let not light see my black and deep desires.
    The eye wink at° the hand; yet let that be   60
    Which the eye fears, when it is done, to see.   *Exit.*

KING.   True, worthy Banquo: he is full so valiant,
    And in his commendations I am fed;°
    It is a banquet to me. Let's after him,
    Whose care is gone before to bid us welcome.   65
    It° is a peerless kinsman.   *Flourish. Exeunt.*

Enter Macbeth's Wife, alone, with a letter.   *I v*

LADY.   [*reads*] "They met me in the day of success; and I have
    learned by the perfect'st report° they have more in them
    than mortal knowledge. When I burned in desire to ques-
    tion them further, they made themselves air, into which
    they vanished. Whiles I stood rapt in the wonder of it, 5
    came missives° from the King, who all-hailed me Thane of
    Cawdor, by which title, before, these weyard sisters saluted
    me, and referred me to the coming on of time with 'Hail,

---

49 From hence i.e. let us go hence (addressed to Macbeth)
49 Inverness location of Macbeth's castle
51 rest repose
52 harbinger forerunner
60 wink at close so as not to see
63 in . . . fed I am nourished by the
praises I bestow on him

66 It he
I v 2 the . . . report Macbeth has presumably made inquiries about the witches' re-
liability
6 missives messengers

King that shalt be!' This have I thought good to deliver°
thee, my dearest partner of greatness, that thou mightst   10
not lose the dues of rejoicing by being ignorant of what
greatness is promised thee. Lay it to thy heart, and
farewell."°

Glamis thou art, and Cawdor, and shalt° be
What thou art promised. Yet do I fear° thy nature.   15
It is too full o' th' milk of human kindness
To catch the nearest° way. Thou wouldst be great,
Art not without ambition, but without
The illness° should attend it. What thou wouldst highly,
That wouldst thou holily;° wouldst not play false,   20
And yet wouldst wrongly win.°
Thou'ldst have, great Glamis, that which cries
"Thus thou must do" if thou have it;
And that which rather thou dost fear to do
Than wishest should be undone.° Hie thee hither,   25
That I may pour my spirits in thine ear
And chastise with the valor of my tongue
All that impedes thee from the golden round°
Which fate and metaphysical° aid doth seem
To have thee crowned withal.°   30

Enter Messenger.

What is your tidings?

MESSENGER.   The King comes here to-night.

LADY.   Thou'rt mad to say it!°
Is not thy master with him? who, were't so,
Would have informed for preparation.°   35

---

9 deliver report to
1-13 They . . . farewell (from the letter's
content it seems that it was written after
the events of I iii but before those of I iv)
14 shalt emphatic (she means to help see
to it)
15 fear have anxieties about
17 nearest i.e. shortest (by killing Duncan)
19 illness wickedness (which)
19-20 What . . . holily what you want
keenly (the throne), you would obtain
fairly
21 wrongly win i.e. win what you have
no right to

22-25 Thou'ldst . . . undone you want a
result that warns you "You must do this" to
get it—and the *this* (i.e. murdering Duncan)
is something you rather shrink from doing
than wish not to be done
28 round crown
29 metaphysical supernatural
30 thee . . . withal crowned you with
33 Thou'rt . . . it (Lady Macbeth responds
with amazement to what seems to be a
further instance of "metaphysical aid"—the
coming of Duncan)
35 for preparation i.e. so that I could prepare for his visit

MESSENGER.   So please you, it is true. Our Thane is coming.
        One of my fellows had the speed of° him,
        Who, almost dead for breath, had scarcely more°
        Than would make up his message.

LADY.   Give him tending;   40
        He brings great news.   *Exit Messenger.*
        The raven° himself is hoarse
        That croaks the fatal entrance° of Duncan
        Under my battlements. Come, you spirits
        That tend on mortal° thoughts, unsex me here,   45
        And fill me from the crown to the toe top-full
        Of direst cruelty. Make thick° my blood;
        Stop up th' access and passage to remorse,°
        That no compunctious° visitings of nature°
        Shake my fell° purpose nor keep peace between   50
        Th' effect and it.° Come to my woman's breasts
        And take° my milk for gall, you murd'ring ministers,°
        Wherever in your sightless° substances
        You wait on° nature's mischief.° Come, thick night,
        And pall thee° in the dunnest° smoke of hell,   55
        That my keen knife see not the wound it makes,
        Nor heaven peep through the blanket of the dark
        To cry "Hold, hold!"

                Enter Macbeth.

        Great Glamis! worthy Cawdor!
        Greater than both, by the all-hail hereafter!°   60
        Thy letters have transported me beyond
        This ignorant° present, and I feel now
        The future in the instant.°

---

37 had . . . of outdistanced
38 more more breath
42 raven (ravens, rooks, and crows were thought to sense, and even announce with their croaking, impending death)
43 entrance perhaps trisyllabic here
45 mortal i.e. deadly
47 thick sluggish, i.e. unresponsive
48 remorse pity
49 compunctious compassionate
49 nature natural sympathy (for a fellow human being)
50 fell savage
50-51 nor . . . it i.e. nor keep such a truce between my intentions and the deed that the deed does not get performed
52 take exchange

52 ministers agents
53 sightless invisible
54 wait on assist
54 nature's mischief (1) the whole network of evil and evil powers in the universe (2) the evil that human nature is capable of (which in turn does harm to that same human nature by dehumanizing it)
55 pall thee shroud yourself
55 dunnest darkest
60 the . . . hereafter i.e. the witches' third "all hail" (I iii 53), which concerns the future
62 ignorant i.e. because it does not know the future (as she now feels she does)
63 instant present moment

MACBETH.   My dearest love,
  Duncan comes here to-night.   65

LADY.   And when goes hence?

MACBETH.   To-morrow, as he purposes.

LADY.   O, never
  Shall sun that morrow see!
  Your face, my Thane, is as a book where men   70
  May read strange matters. To beguile the time,
  Look like the time;° bear welcome in your eye,
  Your hand, your tongue; look like the innocent flower,
  But be the serpent under't. He that's coming
  Must be provided for; and you shall put   75
  This night's great business into my dispatch,°
  Which shall to all our nights and days to come
  Give solely sovereign sway and masterdom.

MACBETH.   We will speak further.

LADY.   Only look up clear.°   80
  To alter favor° ever is to fear.
  Leave all the rest to me.   *Exeunt.*

⌒⌒⌒⌒⌒⌒⌒

Hautboys° and torches. Enter King [Duncan],   *I vi*
Malcolm, Donalbain, Banquo, Lennox,
Macduff, Ross, Angus, and Attendants.

KING.   This castle hath a pleasant seat.°
  The air nimbly and sweetly recommends itself
  Unto our gentle senses.°

BANQUO.   This guest of summer,
  The temple-haunting martlet,° does approve°   5

71-72 **To . . . like the time** to deceive, look normal, i.e. if you plan to put the occasion of Duncan's visit to a tricky and deceptive use, look like a welcoming host, as the occasion demands
76 **dispatch** management
80 **clear** with untroubled face
81 **favor** expression

I vi s.d. Hautboys ancestors of the modern oboe
1 **seat** situation
3 **gentle senses** senses gratified (made gentle) by this pleasure
5 **martlet** martin (bird related to the swallow)
5 **approve** prove

By his loved mansionry° that the heaven's breath
Smells wooingly here. No jutty,° frieze,
Buttress, nor coign of vantage,° but this° bird
Hath made his pendent° bed and procreant° cradle.
Where they most breed and haunt, I have observed   10
The air is delicate.

Enter Lady [Macbeth].

KING. See, see, our honored hostess!
The love that follows us sometime is our trouble,
Which still we thank as love. Herein I teach you
How you shall bid God 'ield us° for your pains   15
And thank us for your trouble.°

LADY. All our service
In every point twice done, and then done double,
Were poor and single° business to contend
Against° those honors deep and broad   20
Wherewith your Majesty loads our house.
For those of old, and the late dignities
Heaped up to° them, we rest° your hermits.°

KING. Where's the Thane of Cawdor?
We coursed° him at the heels and had a purpose   25
To be his purveyor;° but he rides well,
And his great love,° sharp as his spur, hath holp° him
To his home before us. Fair and noble hostess,
We are your guest to-night.

LADY. Your servants ever   30
Have theirs,° themselves, and what is theirs,° in compt,°

---

6 **mansionry** nest-building
7 **jutty** projection
8 **coign of vantage** advantageous corner
7-8 **No . . . this** i.e. in every . . . this
9 **pendent** hanging
9 **procreant** breeding
15 **God . . . us** God yield (reward) me
13-16 **The love . . . trouble** (Duncan speaks either generally or personally, depending on the emphasis given "us," but his point is that as the inconveniences which follow on friendship are accepted gladly because friendship is their cause, so the inconvenience of this visit is to be accepted by Lady Macbeth in the knowledge that its cause is his love for her and her husband)
19 **single** weak
19-20 **contend·Against** offset

23 **to** on top of
23 **rest** remain
23 **hermits** beadsmen, those who prayed (i.e. told their rosary beads) on behalf of others in return for bounties received
25 **coursed** pursued
26 **purveyor** (pronounced here púrveyòr) one who precedes to arrange supplies, (i.e. Duncan would like to have paid Macbeth the complement of being *his* agent instead of vice-versa)
27 **love** (1) for you (Lady Macbeth) (?) (2) for me (his arriving guest) (?)
27 **holp** helped
31 **theirs** their servants
31 **what is theirs** their possessions
31 **in compt** in trust (pronounced "count")

> To make their audit° at your Highness' pleasure,
> Still° to return your own.

KING.   Give me your hand.°
> Conduct me to mine host: we love him highly   35
> And shall continue our graces towards him.
> By your leave, hostess.   *Exeunt.*

❧❧❧

Hautboys. Torches. Enter a Sewer,° and divers Servants with   I vii
dishes and service over the stage. Then enter Macbeth.

MACBETH.   If it were done when 'tis done,° then 'twere well
> It were done quickly. If th' assassination
> Could trammel up° the consequence and catch
> With his surcease success,° that but this blow
> Might be the be-all and the end-all—; here,°   5
> But here upon this bank and shoal of time,°
> We'ld jump° the life to come. But in these cases
> We still° have judgment° here, that° we but teach
> Bloody instructions, which, being taught, return
> To plague th' inventor. This even-handed° justice   10
> Commends° th' ingredience° of our poisoned chalice
> To our own lips. He's here in double trust:
> First, as I am his kinsman and his subject,
> Strong both against the deed; then, as his host,
> Who should against his murderer shut the door,   15
> Not bear the knife myself. Besides, this Duncan

---

32 audit accounting
33 Still always
34 Give . . . hand (spoken as he takes her hand and accompanies her in)
I vii s.d. Sewer butler
1 done . . . done finished with when achieved
3 trammel up confine (as in a trammeling net)
3-4 catch . . . success (1) grasp by means of Duncan's death a happy result (?) (here, "his" refers to Duncan, and "success" is taken in the modern sense) (2) confine and stop what usually follows a murder—e.g. retribution, punishment (?) (here, "his" re-fers to "consequence," "success" is taken to mean succeeding events, and the phrase as a whole is felt to reiterate "trammel up the consequence")
5 here i.e. in this world (without regard to any next world)
6 this . . . time (Macbeth sees earthly life as a sandbank soon washed away)
7 jump risk
8 still always
8 have judgment i.e. receive sentence
8 that so that
10 even-handed impartial
11 Commends applies
11 ingredience ingredients

Hath borne his faculties° so meek, hath been
So clear° in his great office, that his virtues
Will plead like angels, trumpet-tongued against
The deep damnation of his taking-off;   20
And pity, like a naked new-born babe
Striding° the blast, or heaven's cherubin horsed
Upon the sightless° couriers of the air,
Shall blow the horrid deed in every eye°
That tears shall drown the wind.° I have no spur   25
To prick the sides of my intent, but only
Vaulting ambition, which o'erleaps itself
And falls on th' other°—

> *Enter [Lady Macbeth].*

How now? What news?

LADY.   He has almost supped. Why have you left the chamber?   30

MACBETH.   Hath he asked for me?

LADY.   Know you not he has?

MACBETH.   We will proceed no further in this business.
He hath honored me of late, and I have bought°
Golden opinions from all sorts of people,   35
Which would° be worn now in their newest gloss,°
Not cast aside so soon.

LADY.   Was the hope drunk
Wherein you dressed yourself? Hath it slept° since?
And wakes it now to look so green° and pale   40
At what it did so freely? From this time
Such I account thy love. Art thou afeard
To be the same in thine own act and valor
As thou art in desire? Wouldst thou have that°

---

17 faculties regal powers
18 clear blameless
22 Striding bestriding
23 sightless invisible—but perhaps with a further reference to blindness, which is often felt to be an attribute of winds
19-24 plead . . . eye (Macbeth imagines his trial as if in a heavenly court of law, with angels pleading as prosecutors, and pity in the form of a cherub or several cherubin, riding the winds to publicize his crime. The winds serve the cherubin as both horses ("couriers") and trumpets ("blow the horrid deed"))

25 drown . . . wind i.e. like rain
25-28 I . . . other (Macbeth first speaks of himself as rider and his intention as a horse, but then shifts to the image of his ambition as an over-eager rider who, in his zeal to mount, leaps over the saddle and falls off the other side of the horse)
34 bought won (by his feats in battle)
36 would should
36 gloss glow
39 slept i.e. sobered up by sleeping
40 green sickly, i.e. hung-over
44 that i.e. the crown

Which thou esteem'st the ornament of life,   45
And live a coward in thine own esteem?
Letting "I dare not" wait upon° "I would,"
Like the poor cat i' th' adage.°

MACBETH.   Prithee peace!
I dare do all that may become a man;   50
Who dares do more is none.°

LADY.   What beast was't then
That made you break° this enterprise to me?
When you durst do it, then you were a man;
And to be more than what you were, you would   55
Be so much more the man. Nor time nor place
Did then adhere,° and yet you would make both.°
They have made themselves, and that their° fitness now
Does unmake you. I have given suck, and know
How tender 'tis to love the babe that milks me: 60
I would, while it was smiling in my face,
Have plucked my nipple from his boneless gums
And dashed the brains out, had I so sworn
As you have done to this.

MACBETH.   If we should fail?   65

LADY.   We fail?
But° screw your courage to the sticking place°
And we'll not fail. When Duncan is asleep
(Whereto the rather° shall his day's hard journey
Soundly invite him), his two chamberlains   70
Will I with wine and wassail° so convince°

---

47   wait upon constantly follow
48   cat . . . adage ("the cat would eat fish but would not wet her feet")
51   none not a man, i.e. a beast
53   break broach
57   adhere suit
38-57   Was . . . both (Lady Macbeth's accounts of her husband's earlier resolution in 38-39 and 52-57 suggest that there may have been a conversation between them to which we have not been witness, possibly after scene v. On the other hand, since they know by that time that Duncan is coming and she has openly boasted he is never to leave (I v 68ff), how are we to account for her assertion here in 56-57 that time and place were not (when they talked) propitious? Doubtless the contradiction can be glossed over by saying that she now re-fers back to (what she took to be the murderous implication of) his letter before Duncan's visit was known and when time and place, therefore, truly did *not* "adhere"; it seems equally plausible to suppose that we have here a slight temporal blurring of a sort that is often characteristic of Shakespeare; there is no time when an interview faithful to just these circumstances can logically have taken place, but dramatically and practically it did so)
58   that their their very
67   But only
67   sticking place notch (for holding a crossbow string taut)
69   the rather all the more
71   wassail carousing
71   convince overpower

That memory, the warder of the brain,
Shall be a fume, and the receipt of reason
A limbeck only.° When in swinish° sleep
Their drenchèd natures lie as in a death,   75
What cannot you and I perform upon
Th' unguarded Duncan? what not put upon
His spongy° officers, who shall bear the guilt
Of our great quell?°

MACBETH.   Bring forth men-children only;   80
For thy undaunted mettle° should compose
Nothing but males. Will it not be received,°
When we have marked with blood those sleepy two
Of his own chamber and used their very daggers,
That they have done't?   85

LADY.   Who dares receive it other,°
As° we shall make our griefs and clamor roar
Upon his death?

MACBETH.   I am settled and bend up°
Each corporal agent° to this terrible feat.   90
Away, and mock the time° with fairest show;
False face must hide what the false heart doth know.

Exeunt.

〜〜〜〜〜〜

Enter Banquo, and Fleance, with a torch before him.   II i

BANQUO.   How goes the night, boy?

FLEANCE.   The moon is down; I have not heard the clock.

BANQUO.   And she goes down at twelve.

72-74 **memory . . . only** memory (thought
of as seated at the base of the skull, with
reason just above it) will be overcome by
the fumes of the wine and the cavity ("receipt," i.e. receptacle) where reason sits
will be filled with them like a distilling
vessel ("limbeck") (by "a fume," it is probable that Shakespeare intended *afume* [*like
afire, aflame,* etc.])
74 **swinish** i.e. because heavy and snorting

78 **spongy** sodden
79 **quell** killing
81 **mettle** spirit (with pun on metal)
82 **received** interpreted
86 **other** otherwise
87 **As** i.e. considering the way
89 **bend up** (as a bow or crossbow)
90 **corporal agent** physical agency
91 **mock the time** see note I v 71-72

FLEANCE.   I take't, 'tis later, sir.

BANQUO.   Hold, take my sword.   5
  There's husbandry° in heaven;
  Their candles are all out. Take thee that° too.
  A heavy summons° lies like lead upon me,
  And yet I would not sleep.
  Merciful powers, restrain in me the cursèd thoughts   10
  That nature gives way° to in repose.

   Enter Macbeth, and a Servant with a torch.

  Give me my sword: who's there?

MACBETH.   A friend.

BANQUO.   What, sir, not yet at rest? The King's abed.
  He hath been in unusual pleasure   15
  And sent forth great largess to your offices.°
  This diamond he greets your wife withal°
  By the name of most kind hostess,
  And shut up° in measureless content.

MACBETH.   Being unprepared,   20
  Our will became the servant to defect,
  Which else should free have wrought.°

BANQUO.   All's well.
  I dreamt last night of the three weyard sisters.
  To you they have showed some truth.   25

MACBETH.   I think not of them.
  Yet when we can entreat an hour to serve,°
  We would spend it in some words upon that business,
  If you would grant the time.

BANQUO.   At your kind'st leisure.   30

MACBETH.   If you shall cleave to my consent,
  When 'tis,° it shall make honor for you.

II i 6 **husbandry** economy
7 **that** his dagger (?)
8 **summons** (to sleep)
11 **way** access (through evil dreams)
16 **largess . . . offices** i.e. gifts to your household servants
17 **withal** with
19 **shut up** (1) concluded (?) (2) retired behind closed doors (?)
20-22 **Being . . . wrought** not being prepared for his visit, our wish to please him, which otherwise would have been free to express itself fully, was limited by our deficiencies
27 **serve** serve the purpose, i.e. permit us to confer
31-32 **cleave . . . When 'tis** (1) go along with my counsel, when we have our talk (?) (2) stick with my following, when the time comes (?) (Macbeth may be consciously ambiguous)

BANQUO.   So I lose none
    In seeking to augment it,° but still° keep
    My bosom franchised° and allegiance clear,   35
    I shall be counselled.

MACBETH.   Good repose the while.

BANQUO.   Thanks, sir. The like to you.

                            Exeunt Banquo [and Fleance].

MACBETH.   Go bid thy mistress, when my drink° is ready,
    She strike upon the bell. Get thee to bed.   *Exit [Servant].* 40
    Is this a dagger which I see before me,
    The handle toward my hand? Come, let me clutch thee!
    I have thee not, and yet I see thee still.
    Art thou not, fatal° vision, sensible°
    To feeling as to sight? or art thou but   45
    A dagger of the mind, a false creation
    Proceeding from the heat-oppressèd brain?
    I see thee yet, in form as palpable
    As this which now I draw.
    Thou marshall'st me° the way that I was going,   50
    And such an instrument I was to use.
    Mine eyes are made the fools o' th' other senses,
    Or else worth all the rest.° I see thee still,
    And on thy blade and dudgeon° gouts° of blood,
    Which was not so before. There's no such thing.   55
    It is the bloody business which informs°
    Thus to mine eyes. Now o'er the one half-world
    Nature seems dead, and wicked dreams abuse°
    The curtained° sleep. Witchcraft celebrates
    Pale Hecate's° offerings; and withered Murder,   60
    Alarumed° by his sentinel, the wolf,

33-34 So . . . it provided that I lose no honor (honorableness) in augmenting my honor (rank and title)
34 still always
35 franchised freed from guilt
39 drink see II ii 1
44 fatal (1) sent by fate (2) deadly
44 sensible perceptible
50 Thou . . . me you direct me (as an officer marshalls soldiers for a battle)
52-53 Mine . . . rest either my eyes are mistaken in seeing the dagger and are therefore laughed at and made fools of by my other senses as visionaries always are by sane men, or else the vision my eyes see is real and so they are worth all my other senses put together
54 dudgeon hilt
54 gouts drops
56 informs (1) takes form (?) (2) misinforms (?)
58 abuse deceive (see 10-11)
59 curtained (because at night the bed curtains were drawn)
60 Hecate Greek goddess regarded in Shakespeare's day as a goddess of witchcraft (pronounced Hékit)
61 Alarumed alerted to action

Whose howl's his watch,° thus with his stealthy pace,
With Tarquin's ravishing strides,° towards his design
Moves like a ghost. Thou sure and firm-set earth,
Hear not my steps which way they walk, for fear   65
Thy very stones prate of my whereabout
And take the present horror° from the time,
Which now suits with it. Whiles I threat, he lives;
Words to the heat of deeds too cold breath gives.°

                                        A bell rings.

I go, and it is done. The bell invites me.   70
Hear it not, Duncan, for it is a knell
That summons thee to heaven, or to hell.   *Exit.*

᪄᪄᪄᪄᪄᪄᪄᪄

                Enter Lady [Macbeth].   II ii

LADY.   That° which hath made them drunk hath made me bold;
        What hath quenched them hath given me fire.
        Hark! Peace! It was the owl° that shrieked,
        The fatal bellman° which gives the stern'st good-night.
        He is about it.° The doors are open,   5
        And the surfeited° grooms do mock their charge°
        With snores. I have drugged their possets,°
        That death and nature do contend about them
        Whether they live or die.°

---

62 **his watch** ("watch" may mean either watchman, watchword, or timepiece, and "his" may refer to "wolf" or to "Murder," but the point is clear that the wolf's howl signals to the murderer that it is time to carry out his design)
63 **With . . . strides** i.e. with the swift silent movements of a man stealing upon a woman to rape her (in Roman legend, Sextus Tarquin, son of the tyrant Tarquin the Proud, raped a chaste Roman matron named Lucretia, who immediately committed suicide. Her husband and friends then drove the Tarquins from Rome and established the Roman Republic; see Shakespeare's poem *The Rape of Lucrece*)
67 **the . . . horror** i.e. the absolute stillness
69 **Words . . . gives** i.e. words tend to cool action (like blowing on hot food)

II ii 1 **That** i.e. a bedtime drink (see 7, "possets")
3 **owl** (like the raven's croak [see I v 42], the owl's hoot was supposed to bode death)
4 **bellman** (condemned prisoners were visited by the town crier, the bellman, at midnight before their execution and given a last exhortation or farewell)
5 **about it** i.e. performing the murder right now
6 **surfeited** sated with food and drink
6 **mock . . . charge** defy their duty
7 **possets** hot curdled drinks made with milk and wine or milk and ale
8-9 **death . . . die** their condition is such that death claims them for dead, nature for alive

MACBETH. [*within*] Who's there? What, ho?   10

LADY.   Alack, I am afraid they have awaked,
And 'tis not done! Th' attempt, and not the deed,
Confounds° us. Hark! I laid their daggers ready—
He could not miss 'em. Had he not resembled
My father as he slept, I had done't.   15

Enter Macbeth.

My husband!

MACBETH.   I have done the deed.
Didst thou not hear a noise?

LADY.   I heard the owl scream and the crickets cry.
Did not you speak?   20

MACBETH.   When?

LADY.   Now.

MACBETH.   As I descended?

LADY.   Ay.

MACBETH.   Hark! Who lies i' th' second chamber?   25

LADY.   Donalbain.

MACBETH.   This is a sorry° sight.

LADY.   A foolish thought, to say a sorry sight.

MACBETH.   There's one did laugh in's sleep,
And one cried "Murder" that° they did wake each other.   30
I stood and heard them. But they did say their prayers
And addressed them again to sleep.

LADY.   There are two lodged together.

MACBETH.   One cried "God bless us!" and "Amen!" the other,
As they had seen me with these hangman's° hands.   35
List'ning their fear, I could not say "Amen!"
When they did say "God bless us!"

LADY.   Consider it not so deeply.

---

13 Confounds ruins
27 sorry miserable (Macbeth evidently looks here at his hands—or perhaps only at one hand, the other still held behind him clasping the daggers; this would explain why Lady Macbeth does not become aware of the daggers till 57, at which time we may imagine him thrusting the other hand forth, with very powerful stage effect, as she urges him to wash)
30 that so that
35 hangman's i.e. executioner's

MACBETH.   But wherefore could not I pronounce "Amen"?
  I had most need of blessing, and "Amen" stuck in my throat. 40

LADY.   These deeds must not be thought
  After° these ways; so, it will make us mad.

MACBETH.   Methought I heard a voice cry "Sleep no more!
  Macbeth does murder sleep"—the innocent sleep,
  Sleep that knits up the ravelled sleave of care,°   45
  The death of each day's life, sore labor's bath,°
  Balm of hurt minds, great nature's second course,°
  Chief nourisher in life's feast.

LADY.   What do you mean?

MACBETH.   Still it cried "Sleep no more!" to all the house!   50
  "Glamis hath murdered sleep, and therefore Cawdor
  Shall sleep no more, Macbeth shall sleep no more."

LADY.   Who was it that thus cried? Why, worthy Thane,
  You do unbend° your noble strength to think
  So brainsickly of things. Go get some water   55
  And wash this filthy witness° from your hand.°
  Why did you bring these daggers from the place?
  They must lie there: go carry them and smear
  The sleepy grooms with blood.

MACBETH.   I'll go no more.   60
  I am afraid to think what I have done;
  Look on't again I dare not.

LADY.   Infirm of purpose!
  Give me the daggers. The sleeping and the dead
  Are but as pictures. 'Tis the eye of childhood   65
  That fears a painted devil. If he° do bleed,
  I'll gild° the faces of the grooms withal,°
  For it must seem their guilt.°   *Exit. Knock within.*

41-42 thought After reflected on in
45 knits . . . care (during the day life's thread is raveled out by "care" into its separate tiny filaments or "sleaves," then is knit up again at night by "sleep")
46 sore . . . bath soothing like a warm bath after hard work
47 second course i.e. the main course of life's feast
54 unbend loosen (see I vii 89-90)
56 witness evidence

55-56 Go . . . hand (Macbeth's reaction to this advice, which he already knows is fatuous, may be to bring the daggers from behind his back; at any rate, his wife suddenly forgets her interest in his going to wash in favor of returning the daggers and smearing the grooms)
66 he Duncan
67 gild stain
67 withal with it
68 guilt with pun on "gilt" (see 67)

MACBETH.   Whence is that knocking?
    How is't with me when every noise appals me?   70
    What hands are here? Ha! they pluck out mine eyes.
    Will all great Neptune's ocean wash this blood
    Clean from my hand? No, this my hand will rather
    The multitudinous seas incarnadine,°
    Making the green one° red.   75

               Enter Lady [Macbeth].

LADY.   My hands are of your color, but I shame
    To wear a heart so white.
    (*Knock.*) I hear a knocking at the south entry.
    Retire we to our chamber:
    A little water clears us of this deed.   80
    How easy is it then! Your constancy
    Hath left you unattended.°
    (*Knock.*) Hark! more knocking.
    Get on your nightgown,° lest occasion call us
    And show us to be watchers.° Be not lost   85
    So poorly° in your thoughts.

MACBETH.   To know my deed,
    'Twere best not know myself.°   *Knock.*
    Wake Duncan with thy knocking!
    I would thou couldst.   *Exeunt.* 90

                    ❧

           Enter a Porter. Knocking within.   II iii

PORTER.   Here's a knocking indeed! If a man were porter of
    hell gate, he should° have old° turning the key. (*Knock.*)
    Knock, knock, knock. Who's there, i' th' name of Belze-
    bub?° Here's a farmer that hanged himself on th' expecta-

---

74 **incarnadine** redden
75 **one** i.e. all, uniformly
81-82 **Your . . . unattended** your usual firmness has abandoned you
84 **nightgown** dressing gown
85 **watchers** i.e. awake
86 **poorly** weakly
87-88 **To . . . myself** (1) if it means facing my deed, better not be conscious at all

(?) (2) to penetrate the deed I have done to its depths can only be done by giving up my selfhood, i.e. by not knowing (a) the self I have formerly been or (b) the self that a man has as man (?)
II iii 2 should would
2 **old** much
3-4 **Belzebub** Beelzebub

tion° of plenty. Come in time!° Have napkins° enow° about 5
you; here you'll sweat for't. (*Knock.*) Knock, knock. Who's
there, in th' other devil's name? Faith, here's an equivocator,° that could swear in both the scales against either
scale; who committed treason enough for God's sake,° yet
could not equivocate to heaven. O come in, equivocator. 10
(*Knock.*) Knock, knock, knock. Who's there? Faith, here's
an English tailor come hither for stealing out of a French
hose.° Come in, tailor. Here you may roast your goose.°
(*Knock.*) Knock, knock. Never at quiet! What are you?—
But this place is too cold for hell. I'll devil-porter it no 15
further. I had thought to have let in some of all professions
that go the primrose way to th' everlasting bonfire. (*Knock.*)
Anon, anon! [*Opens the way.*] I pray you remember° the
porter.

    Enter Macduff and Lennox.

MACDUFF.   Was it so late, friend, ere you went to bed,   20
    That you do lie so late?

___

4-5 expectation forecast (the farmer hanged himself because, having hoarded for a shortage, which would have enabled him to make a big profit from the needs of the hungry, the actual forecast was for abundance, which would send the price plunging)
5 Come in time (we follow the Folio, which may be taken to mean either "You are come in good time, you are here early, as a sinner like you ought to be," or, imperatively, "Come early," "Come in good season, for you've got a long sweat ahead"; Dover Wilson's emendation to "Come in, time-server" is, however, tempting because it establishes a parallel to "O come in, equivocator" and "Come in, tailor," and also, as he says, creates "an epithet appropriate to all farmers, who must serve Time in its changes of seasons and caprices of weather, and to this farmer in its special sense of one who adapts his conduct to the time with an eye to the main chance")
5 napkins handkerchiefs
5 enow enough
7-8 equivocator (this is a possible allusion to the practice of swearing oaths with mental reservations, which enabled one to swear on both sides of any question—"in both the scales"—and which had been illustrated recently at the trial of the Jesuit Henry Garnet for complicity in the Gunpowder Plot; whether or not there is a topical reference, "equivocation" describes one aspect of Macbeth's experience with the witches and of the new order he tries to establish on their shaky prophecies; see V v 45-47)
9 for . . . sake (this describes the treason from the point of view of the plotters, who believed their purpose to be divinely sanctioned—entered into "for God's sake"—and is also the porter's oath—"for God's sake!" Much of the wry flavor of the porter's speech comes from his using stock phrases, empty counters, in contexts where they suddenly assume explicit meanings—e.g. "in the devil's name" (3-4, 7), "sweat for it" (6), "for God's sake" (9), "hot as hell" (15), etc.)
12-13 for . . . hose (habituated to stealing scraps of cloth while making the old loose-fitting style of hose, he was caught when trying to do the same with the tight-fitting new French style; there is probably a passing glance, too, at the receptacle in which a tailor stored his scraps, which was called his "hell")
13 roast . . . goose heat your pressing iron, called goose from its shape (but probably with a pun on goose as a venereal disease for which heat was the treatment)
4-13 Here's . . . goose the porter imagines a variety of appropriate candidates for hell-gate
18 remember (with a tip)

PORTER.   Faith, sir, we were carousing till the second cock;°
and drink, sir, is a great provoker of three things.

MACDUFF.   What three things does drink especially provoke?

PORTER.   Marry, sir, nose-painting,° sleep, and urine. Lechery, 25
sir, it provokes, and unprovokes: it provokes the desire,
but it takes away the performance. Therefore much drink
may be said to be an equivocator with lechery: it makes
him, and it mars him; it sets him on, and it takes him off;
it persuades him, and disheartens him; makes him stand 30
to, and not stand to; in conclusion, equivocates him in a
sleep,° and, giving him the lie,° leaves him.

MACDUFF.   I believe drink gave thee the lie last night.

PORTER.   That it did, sir, i' the very throat° on me; but I re-
quited him for his lie; and, I think, being too strong for 35
him, though he took up my legs sometime, yet I made a
shift to cast° him.

MACDUFF.   Is thy master stirring?

Enter Macbeth.

Our knocking has awaked him: here he comes.

LENNOX.   Good morrow, noble sir.   40

MACBETH.   Good morrow, both.

MACDUFF.   Is the King stirring, worthy Thane?

MACBETH.   Not yet.

MACDUFF.   He did command me to call timely° on him;
I have almost slipped° the hour.   45

MACBETH.   I'll bring you to him.

MACDUFF.   I know this is a joyful trouble to you;
But yet 'tis one.

MACBETH.   The labor we delight in physics° pain.
This is the door.   50

---

22 **second cock** i.e. second cock-crow, an
event conventionally established as taking
place at 3 a.m.
25 **nose-painting** a red nose
31-32 **in a sleep** (1) i.e. by incapacitating
him through drowsiness (?) (2) by an emis-
sion in sleep (?)
32 **giving . . . lie** calling him a liar (with
a pun on "lie" in the sense of unable to
stand)

34 **throat** (in allusion to the challenge,
"You lie in your throat!")
37 **cast** i.e. throw (as one wrestler throws
another), but with a pun on casting up,
vomiting
44 **timely** early
45 **slipped** let slip
49 **physics** cures

MACDUFF.   I'll make so bold to call, for 'tis my limited° service.

Exit Macduff.

LENNOX.   Goes the King hence to-day?

MACBETH.   He does; he did appoint so.

LENNOX.   The night has been unruly.
Where we lay, our chimneys were blown down;   55
And, as they say, lamentings heard i' th' air,
Strange screams of death,
And prophesying, with accents terrible,
Of dire combustion° and confused events
New hatched to th' woeful time.   60
The obscure bird° clamored the livelong night.
Some say the earth was feverous
And did shake.

MACBETH.   'Twas a rough° night.

LENNOX.   My young remembrance cannot parallel   65
A fellow° to it.

Enter Macduff.

MACDUFF.   O horror, horror, horror!
Tongue nor heart cannot conceive nor name thee!

MACBETH AND LENNOX.   What's the matter?

MACDUFF.   Confusion° now hath made his masterpiece: 70
Most sacrilegious murder hath broke ope
The Lord's anointed temple° and stole thence
The life o' th' building!

MACBETH.   What is't you say? the life?

LENNOX.   Mean you his Majesty?   75

MACDUFF.   Approach the chamber and destroy your sight°
With a new Gorgon. Do not bid me speak.
See, and then speak yourselves. Awake, awake!

Exeunt Macbeth and Lennox.

Ring the alarum bell! Murder and treason!
Banquo and Donalbain! Malcolm, awake!   80
Shake off this downy sleep, death's counterfeit,

---

51 **limited** appointed
59 **combustion** tumult
61 **obscure bird** bird of darkness, i.e. the owl
64 **rough** stormy
65-66 **parallel A fellow** find an equal

70 **Confusion** destruction
72 **The . . . temple** the sacred body of the king
76 **destroy . . . sight** (as all did who looked at the Gorgon Medusa, the sight of whom turned men to stone)

And look on death itself. Up, up, and see
The great doom's image.° Malcolm! Banquo!
As from your graves rise up and walk like sprites°
To countenance° this horror. Ring the bell!   *Bell rings.* 85

Enter Lady [Macbeth].

LADY.   What's the business,
That such a hideous trumpet calls to parley
The sleepers of the house? Speak, speak!

MACDUFF.   O gentle lady,
'Tis not for you to hear what I can speak: 90
The repetition in a woman's ear
Would murder as it fell.

Enter Banquo.

O Banquo, Banquo, our royal master's murdered!

LADY.   Woe, alas!
What, in our house?   95

BANQUO.   Too cruel anywhere.
Dear Duff, I prithee contradict thyself
And say it is not so.

Enter Macbeth, Lennox, and Ross.

MACBETH.   Had I but died an hour before this chance,
I had lived a blessèd time; for from this instant   100
There's nothing serious in mortality:°
All is but toys.° Renown and grace is dead,
The wine of life is drawn, and the mere lees°
Is left this vault° to brag of.

Enter Malcolm and Donalbain.

DONALBAIN.   What is amiss?   105

MACBETH.   You are,° and do not know't.
The spring, the head, the fountain of your blood
Is stopped, the very source of it is stopped.

MACDUFF.   Your royal father's murdered.

---

83 **great . . . image** image of Doomsday
itself
84 **sprites** spirits
85 **countenance** (1) suit (2) behold
101 **serious in mortality** worthwhile in life
102 **toys** trifles

103 **lees** dregs
104 **vault** (1) wine cellar (2) earth, with its
vault, the sky
106 **You are** i.e. you are amiss, for you
are missing, lacking, your father

MALCOLM.   O, by whom?   110

LENNOX.   Those of his chamber, as it seemed, had done't.
        Their hands and faces were all badged° with blood;
        So were their daggers, which unwiped we found
        Upon their pillows. They stared and were distracted.
        No man's life was to be trusted with them.   115

MACBETH.   O, yet I do repent me of my fury
        That I did kill them.

MACDUFF.   Wherefore did you so?

MACBETH.   Who can be wise, amazed,° temp'rate and furious,
        Loyal and neutral, in a moment? No man.   120
        The expedition° of my violent love
        Outrun° the pauser, reason. Here lay Duncan,
        His silver skin laced° with his golden blood;
        And his gashed stabs looked like a breach in nature
        For ruin's wasteful entrance:° there, the murderers,   125
        Steeped in the colors of their trade, their daggers
        Unmannerly breeched° with gore. Who could refrain
        That had a heart to love, and in that heart
        Courage to make's love known?

LADY.   Help me hence, ho!   130

MACDUFF.   Look to the lady.

MALCOLM.   [*aside to Donalbain*] Why do we hold our tongues,
        That most may claim this argument° for ours?

DONALBAIN.   [*to Malcolm*] What should be spoken here,
        Where our fate, hid in an auger hole,°   135
        May rush and seize us? Let's away:
        Our tears are not yet brewed.°

MALCOLM.   [*to Donalbain*] Nor our strong sorrow
        Upon the foot of motion.°

BANQUO.   Look to the lady.   [*Lady Macbeth is carried out.*] 140
        And when we have our naked frailties hid,°

---

112 **badged** marked
119 **amazed** confused
121 **expedition** speed
122 **Outrun** outran
123 **laced** i.e. (1) like lace (?) (2) cross-wise, like lacings (?)
124-25 **breach . . . entrance** i.e. such an opening as attackers would make in the walls of a city

127 **Unmannerly breeched** covered as with breeches—unmannerly because their rightful breeches are their sheaths
133 **argument** subject
135 **auger hole** i.e. any place (however tiny or unsuspected)
137 **brewed** i.e. ready for pouring
139 **Upon . . . motion** i.e. ready to act
141 **frailties hid** bodies clothed

That suffer in exposure, let us meet
And question this most bloody piece of work,
To know it further. Fears and scruples° shake us.
In the great hand of God I stand, and thence   145
Against the undivulged pretense° I fight
Of treasonous malice.

MACDUFF.   And so do I.

ALL.   So all.

MACBETH.   Let's briefly put on manly readiness°   150
And meet i' th' hall together.

ALL.   Well contented.

                 Exeunt [all but Malcolm and Donalbain].

MALCOLM.   What will you do?
Let's not consort with them.
To show an unfelt sorrow is an office   155
Which the false man does easy.
I'll to England.

DONALBAIN.   To Ireland I.
Our separated fortune shall keep us both the safer.
Where we are, there's daggers in men's smiles;   160
The near in blood, the nearer bloody.°

MALCOLM.   This murderous shaft that's shot
Hath not yet lighted, and our safest way
Is to avoid the aim. Therefore to horse,
And let us not be dainty of° leave-taking   165
But shift° away. There's warrant° in that theft
Which steals itself when there's no mercy left.   *Exeunt.*

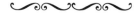

---

144   **scruples**   suspicious
146   **pretense**   plot
150   **manly readiness**   (1) proper clothing
(2) a resolute mood
161   **The near . . . bloody**   the nearer we
are to Duncan in blood (as his heirs), the
nearer we are to being bloodied, i.e. murdered
165   **dainty of**   fastidious in insisting on
166   **shift**   steal
166   **warrant** . justification

Enter Ross with an Old Man.   II i*

OLD MAN.   Threescore and ten I can remember well;
           Within the volume of which time I have seen
           Hours dreadful and things strange, but this sore° night
           Hath trifled former knowings.°

Ross.   Ha, good father,   5
        Thou seest° the heavens, as troubled with man's act,°
        Threatens° his bloody stage. By th' clock 'tis day,
        And yet dark night strangles the travelling lamp.°
        Is't night's predominance,° or the day's shame,°
        That darkness does the face of earth entomb   10
        When living light should kiss it?

OLD MAN.   'Tis unnatural,
           Even like the deed that's done. On Tuesday last
           A falcon, tow'ring in her pride of place,°
           Was by a mousing° owl hawked at° and killed.   15

Ross.   And Duncan's horses
        (A thing most strange and certain),
        Beauteous and swift, the minions° of their race,
        Turned wild in nature, broke their stalls, flung out,
        Contending 'gainst obedience, as they would   20
        Make war with mankind.

OLD MAN.   'Tis said they eat° each other.

Ross.   They did so,
        To th' amazement of mine eyes that looked upon't.

Enter Macduff.

        Here comes the good Macduff.   25
        How goes the world, sir, now?

MACDUFF.   Why, see you not?

Ross.   Is't known who did this more than bloody deed?

II iv 3 **sore** painful
4 **trifled . . . knowings** reduced by former experience of horror to trifles
6 **seest** seest that
6 **act** (1) behavior, especially in this murder (2) life in general—viewed as a stage performance or play
7 **Threatens** ("the heavens" are thought of as singular)
8 **lamp** i.e. the sun
9 **predominance, shame** i.e. owing to the black deed that has been done
14 **tow'ring . . . place** soaring to her pitch (the high point from which she attacks)
15 **mousing** i.e. normally preying on mice
15 **hawked at** preyed on, i.e. the owl changed its nature (like the horses, 16-21)
18 **minions** darlings, i.e. best
22 **eat** ate

MACDUFF. Those that Macbeth hath slain.

ROSS. Alas the day,   30
    What good could they pretend?°

MACDUFF. They were suborned.°
    Malcolm and Donalbain, the King's two sons,
    Are stol'n away and fled, which puts upon them
    Suspicion of the deed.   35

ROSS. 'Gainst nature still.°
    Thriftless ambition, that wilt raven° up
    Thine own live's means!° Then 'tis most like
    The sovereignty will fall upon Macbeth.

MACDUFF. He is already named, and gone to Scone°   40
    To be invested.°

ROSS. Where is Duncan's body?

MACDUFF. Carried to Colmekill,°
    The sacred storehouse of his predecessors
    And guardian of their bones.   45

ROSS. Will you to Scone?

MACDUFF. No, cousin, I'll to Fife.°

ROSS. Well, I will thither.

MACDUFF. Well, may you see things well done there.° Adieu,
    Lest our old robes° sit easier than our new!   50

ROSS. Farewell, father.

OLD MAN. God's benison° go with you,° and with those°
    That would make good of bad, and friends of foes.

Exeunt omnes.

~⌒⌒⌒~

---

31 **good . . . pretend** gain . . . intend
32 **suborned** bribed
36 **'Gainst . . . still** (if, as Ross assumes, Duncan's own sons killed him, this too is an act "against nature," like the behavior of the sun, the owl, and the horses)
37 **raven** devour
38 **Thine . . . means** Your own begetter
40 **Scone** royal city where the Scottish kings were crowned

41 **invested** robed and crowned
43 **Colmekill** Iona, one of the Hebrides
47 **Fife** Macduff's own home
49 **Well . . . there** i.e. may what goes on at Scone prove a good thing for Scotland
50 **old robes** former king (Duncan)
52 **benison** blessing
52 **you** i.e. Macduff (who is absenting himself from the coronation)
52 **those** e.g. Ross (who will attend it)

Enter Banquo.

BANQUO.   Thou hast it now—King, Cawdor, Glamis, all,
As the weyard women promised; and I fear
Thou playedst° most foully for't. Yet it was said
It should not stand° in thy posterity,
But that myself should be the root and father   5
Of many kings. If there come truth from them
(As upon thee, Macbeth, their speeches shine°),
Why, by the verities on thee made good,
May they not be my oracles as well
And set me up in hope? But hush, no more!   10

Sennet° sounded. Enter Macbeth as King, Lady [Macbeth],
Lennox, Ross, Lords, and Attendants.

MACBETH.   Here's our chief guest.

LADY.   If he had been forgotten,
It had been as a gap in our great feast,
And all-thing° unbecoming.

MACBETH.   To-night we hold a solemn° supper, sir,   15
And I'll request your presence.

BANQUO.   Let your Highness
Command upon° me, to the which my duties
Are with a most indissoluble° tie
For ever knit.   20

MACBETH.   Ride you this afternoon?

BANQUO.   Ay, my good lord.

MACBETH.   We should have else desired your good advice
(Which still° hath been both grave and prosperous°)
In this day's council; but we'll take to-morrow.   25
Is't far you ride?

BANQUO.   As far, my lord, as will fill up the time
'Twixt this and supper. Go not my horse the better,°

III i 3 **playedst** see I v 20-21
4 **stand** remain
7 **shine** have radiantly come true (Banquo
may be alluding to the actual glitter of the
crown)
10 s.d. **Sennet** trumpet salute
14 **all-thing** altogether
15 **solemn** formal

18 **Command upon** command
19 **indissoluble** pronounced indíssolùble
24 **still** always
24 **prosperous** i.e. causing affairs to pros-
per
28 **Go . . . better** if my horse does not
better the time usually allowed for such a
distance

I must become a borrower of the night
For a dark hour or twain.   30

MACBETH.   Fail not our feast.

BANQUO.   My lord, I will not.

MACBETH.   We hear our bloody cousins° are bestowed
In England and in Ireland, not confessing
Their cruel parricide, filling their hearers   35
With strange invention.° But of that to-morrow,
When therewithal° we shall have cause of state
Craving us jointly.° Hie you to horse.
Adieu, till you return at night.
Goes Fleance with you?   40

BANQUO.   Ay, my good lord. Our time does call upon's.°

MACBETH.   I wish your horses swift and sure of foot,
And so I do commend you to their backs.
Farewell.   *Exit Banquo.*
Let every man be master of his time   45
Till seven at night. To make society
The sweeter welcome,
We will keep ourself till supper time alone.
While° then, God be with you!
                                    Exeunt Lords [and others].
Sirrah,° a word with you. Attend° those men   50
Our pleasure?

SERVANT.   They are, my lord, without the palace gate.

MACBETH.   Bring them before us.   *Exit Servant.*
To be thus is nothing, but° to be safely thus—
Our fears in° Banquo stick deep,°   55
And in his royalty of nature reigns that
Which would° be feared. 'Tis much he dares;
And to° that dauntless temper of his mind
He hath a wisdom that doth guide his valor
To act in safety. There is none but he   60

---

33 **cousins** Malcolm and Donalbain
36 **invention** lies
37 **therewithal** in addition (to the behavior of Malcolm and Donalbain)
37-38 **cause . . . jointly** matters of state
that require the attention of both of us
41 **Our . . . upon's** i.e. we must be off
49 **While** until

50 **Sirrah** term of address to a menial
50 **Attend** await
54 **but** unless
55 **in** in reference to
55 **stick deep** (1) in my flesh (like thorns)
(?) (2) in his nature (like roots) (?)
57 **would** should
58 **to** in addition to

Whose being I do fear; and under him
My genius° is rebuked,° as it is said
Mark Antony's was by Caesar.° He chid the sisters
When first they put the name of King upon me,
And bade them speak to him. Then, prophet-like,   65
They hailed him father to a line of kings.
Upon my head they placed a fruitless° crown
And put a barren sceptre in my gripe,°
Thence to be wrenched with an unlineal° hand,
No son of mine succeeding. If't be so,   70
For Banquo's issue° have I filed° my mind;
For them the gracious Duncan have I murdered,
Put rancors in the vessel of my peace°
Only for them, and mine eternal jewel°
Given to the common enemy of man°   75
To make them kings—the seeds of Banquo kings.
Rather than so, come, Fate, into the list,°
And champion me to th' utterance!°
Who's there?°

Enter Servant and two Murderers.

Now go to the door and stay there till we call.   80

Exit Servant.

Was it not yesterday we spoke together?

MURDERERS.   It was, so please your Highness.

MACBETH.   Well then,
Now have you considered of my speeches?
Know° that it was he,° in the times past,   85
Which held you so under fortune,°

---

62 genius guardian angel (which every
human being was reputed to have from
birth)
62 rebuked cowed
61-63 under . . . Caesar (see *Antony and
Cleopatra*, II iii 17ff, where a soothsayer
tells Antony that Caesar's fortunes will rise
higher than his: "Therefore, O Antony, stay
not by his side: / Thy demon, that thy spirit
which keeps thee, is / Noble, courageous,
high, unmatchable, / Where Caesar's is not.
But near him, thy angel / Becomes afeard, as
being o'erpower'd; therefore / Make space
enough between you.")
67 fruitless i.e. heirless
68 gripe grasp
69 unlineal i.e. not of my line, my blood
71 issue descendants

71 filed defiled
73 peace thought of as a benign liquid in
a vessel into which Macbeth has now introduced bitter ingredients, "rancors" (see I
vii 10-12)
74 jewel i.e. soul
75 common . . . man i.e. Satan
77 list lists, fields of combat
78 to th' utterance à *outrance*, i.e. to the
death
79 Who's there? (a summons to his servant)
85 Know i.e. now you know
85 he Banquo
86 held . . . fortune kept you from pros-
pering (the Murderers have evidently been
minor retainers or officers in Banquo's ret-
inue or sphere of influence)

Which you thought had been our innocent self.
This I made good° to you in our last conference,
Passed in probation° with you
How you were borne in hand,° how crossed;°   90
The instruments;° who wrought° with them;
And all things else that might
To half a soul° and to a notion° crazed
Say "Thus did Banquo."

1. MURDERER.   You made it known to us.   95

MACBETH.   I did so;
And went further, which is now
Our point of second meeting.
Do you find your patience so predominant
In your nature that you can let this go?°   100
Are you so gospelled° to° pray for this good man
And for his issue, whose heavy hand
Hath bowed you to the grave and beggared
Yours° for ever?

1. MURDERER.   We are men, my liege.   105

MACBETH.   Ay, in the catalogue° ye go for men,
As hounds and greyhounds, mongrels, spaniels, curs,
Shoughs,° water-rugs,° and demi-wolves are clept°
All by the name of dogs. The valued file°
Distinguishes the swift, the slow, the subtle,   110
The housekeeper, the hunter, every one
According to the gift which bounteous nature
Hath in him closed, whereby he does receive
Particular addition, from the bill
That writes them all alike;° and so of men.   115
Now, if you have a station in the file,°

---

88 **good** clear
89 **Passed in probation** reviewed the proofs
90 **borne in hand** manipulated and deceived
90 **crossed** thwarted
91 **instruments** agents
91 **wrought** worked
93 **To . . . soul** even to a halfwit
93 **notion** mind
100 **go** i.e. unrevenged
101 **gospelled** i.e. subject to Gospel admonitions like loving your enemies and turning the other cheek
101 **to** as to

104 **Yours** your issue (see "his issue," 102)
106 **catalogue** generic classification
108 **Shoughs** shaggy dogs (pronounced "shocks")
108 **water-rugs** shaggy water dogs
108 **clept** named
109 **valued file** specific classification (by attributes)
114-15 **Particular . . . alike** i.e. a specific name that distinguishes him from the generic list ("bill") of "dogs"
116 **station . . . file** place in the list

Not i' th' worst rank of manhood, say't;
And I will put that business in your bosoms
Whose execution takes your enemy off,
Grapples you to the heart and love of us,   120
Who wear our health but sickly in° his life,
Which in° his death were perfect.

2. MURDERER.   I am one, my liege,
Whom the vile blows and buffets of the world
Hath° so incensed that I am reckless what I do   125
To spite the world.

1. MURDERER.   And I another,
So weary with disasters, tugged with° fortune,
That I would set° my life on any chance
To mend it or be rid on't.   130

MACBETH.   Both of you know Banquo was your enemy.

MURDERERS.   True, my lord.

MACBETH.   So is he mine, and in such bloody distance°
That every minute of his being thrusts
Against my near'st of life;° and though I could   135
With barefaced power sweep him from my sight
And bid my will avouch° it, yet I must not,
For° certain friends that are both his and mine,
Whose loves I may not drop, but wail° his fall
Who I myself struck down. And thence it is   140
That I to your assistance do make love,
Masking the business from the common eye
For sundry weighty reasons.

2. MURDERER.   We shall, my lord,
Perform what you command us.   145

1. MURDERER.   Though our lives°—

MACBETH.   Your spirits shine through you.
Within this hour at most
I will advise you where to plant yourselves,

---

121 **in** during
122 **in** on
125 **Hath** have
128 **tugged with** mauled by
129 **set** bet, i.e. risk
133 **distance** hostility

135 **near'st of life** vital parts
137 **avouch** justify
138 **For** because of
139 **wail** I must bewail (in public)
146 **Though our lives** (Macbeth cuts short
an assertion of zeal)

Acquaint you with the perfect spy o' th' time,°   150
The moment on't, for't must be done to-night
And something° from the palace (always thought°
That I require a clearness°); and with him,
To leave no rubs nor botches° in the work,
Fleance his son, that keeps him company,   155
Whose absence is no less material to me
Than is his father's, must embrace the fate
Of that dark hour. Resolve yourselves apart;°
I'll come to you anon.

MURDERERS.   We are resolved, my lord.   160

MACBETH.   I'll call upon you straight.° Abide within.
It is concluded. Banquo, thy soul's flight,
If it find heaven, must find it out to-night.   *Exeunt.*

✦✦✦

Enter Macbeth's Lady and a Servant.   III ii

LADY.   Is Banquo gone from court?

SERVANT.   Ay, madam, but returns again to-night.

LADY.   Say to the King I would attend his leisure
For a few words.

SERVANT.   Madam, I will.   *Exit.* 5

LADY.   Naught's had, all's spent,
Where our desire is got without content.
'Tis safer to be that which we destroy°
Than by destruction dwell in doubtful° joy.

Enter Macbeth.

How now, my lord? Why do you keep alone,   10

---

150 perfect . . . time exact observation
("spy") of the favorable moment (perhaps
to be conveyed by the man who is called
"Third Murderer" in III iii)
152 something some distance
152 thought i.e. kept in mind
153 clearness i.e. from any incrimination
154 rubs, botches flaws

158 Resolve . . . apart consider the matter
by yourselves (whether you will do it or
not)
161 straight immediately
III ii 8 that . . . destroy i.e. a murdered
man
9 doubtful apprehensive (but with a
glance at the usual meaning)

Of sorriest° fancies your companions making,
Using° those thoughts which should indeed have died
With them they think on? Things without all° remedy
Should be without regard. What's done is done.

MACBETH.   We have scorched° the snake, not killed it.   15
She'll close° and be herself, whilst our poor malice
Remains in danger of her former tooth.°
But let the frame of things disjoint,
Both the worlds suffer,°
Ere we will eat our meal in fear, and sleep   20
In the affliction of these terrible dreams
That shake us nightly. Better be with the dead,
Whom we, to gain our peace, have sent to peace,
Than on the torture of the mind to lie
In restless ecstasy.°   25
Duncan is in his grave;
After life's fitful fever he sleeps well.
Treason has done his worst: nor steel nor poison,
Malice domestic, foreign levy,° nothing,
Can touch him further.   30

LADY.   Come on.
Gentle my lord, sleek° o'er your rugged looks;
Be bright and jovial among your guests to-night.

MACBETH.   So shall I, love; and so, I pray, be you.
Let your remembrance apply to Banquo;   35
Present him eminence° both with eye and tongue:
Unsafe the while, that we must lave
Our honors in these flattering streams°
And make our faces vizards° to our hearts,
Disguising what they are.   40

LADY.   You must leave this.°

---

11 **sorriest** see note II ii 27
12 **Using** indulging
13 **all** any
15 **scorched** slashed in pieces
16 **close** heal
17 **her . . . tooth** i.e. her tooth, as formerly
18-19 **But . . . suffer** but let the universe
come apart at the joints and both heavens
and earth be ruined
25 **ecstasy** frenzy (for Lady Macbeth's
strikingly similar remark, see 8-9)

29 **foreign levy** i.e. attack by a foreign
nation
32 **sleek** smooth
36 **Present him eminence** honor him
37-38 **Unsafe . . . streams** we are not safe
so long as we must maintain ("lave" means,
literally, to wash) our high estate ("honors")
with flattery
39 **vizards** masks
41 **this** i.e. this kind of mood and talk

MACBETH.   O, full of scorpions is my mind, dear wife!
     Thou know'st that Banquo, and his Fleance, lives.

LADY.   But in them Nature's copy's° not eterne.°

MACBETH.   There's comfort yet; they are assailable.   45
     Then be thou jocund.° Ere the bat hath flown
     His cloistered° flight, ere to black Hecate's° summons
     The shard-borne° beetle with his drowsy hums°
     Hath rung night's yawning peal,°
     There shall be done a deed of dreadful note.   50

LADY.   What's to be done?

MACBETH.   Be innocent of the knowledge, dearest chuck,°
     Till thou applaud the deed. Come, seeling° night,
     Scarf up° the tender eye of pitiful° day,
     And with thy bloody and invisible hand   55
     Cancel and tear to pieces that great bond°
     Which keeps me pale. Light thickens,°
     And the crow makes wing to th' rooky° wood.
     Good things of day begin to droop and drowse,
     Whiles night's black agents to their preys do rouse.   60
     Thou marvell'st at my words, but hold thee still;
     Things bad begun make strong themselves by ill.
     So prithee go with me.   *Exeunt.*

---

44 copy ("copy" here may have any one, or all three, of the following meanings, but perhaps especially the third): (1) copie, or plenty—the vitality "Nature" supplies that keeps us alive (2) pattern—in the sense of a design that "Nature" impresses, as a potter may do in clay (3) copyhold, i.e. a lease (on life)
44 eterne eternal
46 jocund happy
47 cloistered i.e. within walls
47 Hecate see note II i 60
48 shard-borne i.e. born from dung (often mistakenly rendered as "borne on scaly wings"—see OED, "shard," sb. 2, and "shard-born, -borne")
48 hums (the common dung beetle flies mostly after sunset making a loud humming noise)
49 night's . . . peal i.e. night's sleepy curfew

52 chuck i.e. chick, a term of endearment
53 seeling (a term from falconry for the practice of sewing a hawk's eyelids closed to keep him in the dark and thus control him)
54 Scarf up blindfold
54 pitiful because it would show pity
56 bond (1) the bond or leasehold (see 44) that ties Banquo and Fleance to life (?) (2) the bond of human beings to each other that the murder will betray (?) (3) the promise that Banquo's heirs are to inherit the throne (?)
57 thickens dims
58 rooky crow-filled (because the wood is their nocturnal hunting ground, but with the further implication that, as carrion-eaters, they wait for the murder to come: see I v 42)

Enter three Murderers.

1. MURDERER.   But who did bid thee join with us?

3. MURDERER.   Macbeth.

2. MURDERER.   He° needs not our mistrust, since he delivers°
    Our offices° and what we have to do
    To the direction just.°   5

1. MURDERER.   Then stand with us.
    The west yet glimmers with some streaks of day.
    Now spurs the lated° traveller apace
    To gain the timely° inn, and near approaches
    The subject of our watch.   10

3. MURDERER.   Hark, I hear horses.

BANQUO.   (*within*) Give us a light there,° ho!

2. MURDERER.   Then 'tis he;
    The rest that are within the note of expectation°
    Already are i' th' court.   15

1. MURDERER.   His horses go about.

3. MURDERER.   Almost a mile; but he does usually,
    So all men do, from hence to th' palace gate
    Make it their walk.°

Enter Banquo and Fleance, with a torch.

2. MURDERER.   A light, a light!   20

3. MURDERER.   'Tis he.

1. MURDERER.   Stand to't.°

BANQUO.   It will be rain to-night.

1. MURDERER.   Let it° come down!

III iii 3 **He** the third murderer
3 delivers states
4 offices duties
5 To . . . just exactly according to our instructions
8 lated belated
9 timely i.e. because night approaches
12 Give . . . there (the murderers are evidently waylaying Banquo [in a wood?] near Macbeth's palace, and Banquo, at his approach, calls for a palace servant to come with a torch for him and Fleance and take the horses to stable)
14 note of expectation list of invited guests

16-19 His . . . walk (the first murderer hears the noise of the horses going off and is reassured by the third murderer that Banquo will pass by them; "Almost a mile" may describe the distance to the stables or to the palace)
22 Stand to't be ready
24 it i.e. the rain—but also the rain of blows (?) (Shakespeare may have wanted the weather reference to remind us of the witches—"In thunder, lightning, or in rain" —who, in their effects, are present here)

BANQUO.   O, treachery!   25
    Fly, good Fleance, fly, fly, fly!   [*Exit Fleance.*]
    Thou mayst revenge—O slave!   [*Banquo slain.*]

3. MURDERER.   Who did strike out the light?

1. MURDERER.   Was't not the way?°

3. MURDERER.   There's but one down: the son is fled.   30

2. MURDERER.   We have lost
Best half of our affair.

1. MURDERER.   Well, let's away, and say how much is done.

                                               Exeunt.

Banquet prepared. Enter Macbeth, Lady [Macbeth],   III iv
   Ross, Lennox, Lords, and Attendants.

MACBETH.   You know your own degrees°—sit down:
    At first and last,° the hearty welcome.

LORDS.   Thanks to your Majesty.

MACBETH.   Ourself will mingle with society°
    And play the humble host.   5
    Our hostess keeps her state,° but in best time
    We will require° her welcome.

LADY.   Pronounce it for me, sir, to all our friends,
    For my heart speaks they are welcome.

            Enter First Murderer.

MACBETH.   See, they encounter° thee with their hearts' thanks.   10
    Both sides are even.° Here I'll sit i' th' midst.

---

29 way i.e. right thing to do
III iv 1 degrees ranks, according to which
seating was arranged
2 At . . . last from first to last
4 society the guests
6 state throne ("chairs of state," in this
case thrones, are evidently set up for the
king and queen on one side or other of
the stage, while the table for the guests
occupies the middle—Lady Macbeth will
stay on her throne—it was usual for royalty
to dine separately—but Macbeth will sit at
table with the guests)

7 require request
10 encounter respond to
11 Both . . . even (this may signify that
the guests' "thanks" and Lady Macbeth's
"welcome" equal each other [see "encounter," 10] or simply that both sides of the
table are evenly filled. In either case, the
rest of the line is the means by which
Shakespeare indicates to the audience Macbeth's seat at table, which will shortly be
taken by the ghost of murdered Banquo)

Be large° in mirth; anon we'll drink a measure
The table round.° [*Goes to Murderer.*] There's blood upon
   thy face.

MURDERER.   'Tis Banquo's then.

MACBETH.   'Tis better thee without than he within.°   15
   Is he dispatched?

MURDERER.   My lord, his throat is cut: that I did for him.

MACBETH.   Thou art the best o' th' cut-throats.
   Yet he's good that did the like for Fleance:
   If thou didst it, thou art the nonpareil.°   20

MURDERER.   Most royal sir,
   Fleance is scaped.

MACBETH.   [*aside*] Then comes my fit again.
   I had else been perfect;
   Whole as the marble, founded° as the rock,   25
   As broad and general° as the casing° air.
   But now I am cabined, cribbed, confined, bound in
   To saucy° doubts and fears.°—But Banquo's safe?

MURDERER.   Ay, my good lord. Safe in a ditch he bides,
   With twenty trenchèd° gashes on his head,   30
   The least a death to nature.

MACBETH.   Thanks for that.—
   [*Aside*] There the grown serpent lies; the worm° that's fled
   Hath nature that in time will venom breed,
   No teeth for th' present.—Get thee gone. To-morrow   35
   We'll hear ourselves° again.   *Exit Murderer.*

LADY.   My royal lord,
   You do not give the cheer.° The feast is sold°
   That is not° often vouched,° while 'tis a-making,
   'Tis° given with welcome. To feed° were best at home;   40

---

12 **large** uninhibited
12-13 **drink . . . round** drink from a mutual cup as it passes about the table (in sign of fellowship)
15 **thee . . . within** *on* you than *in* him
20 **nonpareil** paragon (of murderers)
25 **founded** fixed firmly
26 **broad and general** unconfined
26 **casing** encasing
28 **saucy** insolent (as threatening a king)
27-28 **cabined . . . fears** i.e. boxed in by anxieties and fears (lest Duncan's murder be uncovered)

30 **trenched** trench-like, i.e. deep
33 **worm** young serpent
36 **hear ourselves** confer
38 **cheer** a sense of hospitality
38 **sold** i.e. instead of given
39 **That is not** unless it is
39 **vouched** certified
40 **'Tis** i.e. that it is
40 **To feed** i.e. merely to eat

From thence,° the sauce to meat° is ceremony:
Meeting° were bare° without it.

Enter the Ghost of Banquo, and sits in Macbeth's place.

MACBETH.   Sweet remembrancer!°
Now good digestion wait on° appetite,
And health on both!   45

LENNOX.   May't please your Highness sit.

MACBETH.   Here had we° now our country's honor,° roofed,°
Were the graced° person of our Banquo present—
Who may I rather challenge for unkindness
Than pity for mischance!°   50

ROSS.   His absence, sir,
Lays blame upon° his promise. Please't your Highness
To grace us with your royal company?

MACBETH.   The table's full.

LENNOX.   Here is a place reserved, sir.°   55

MACBETH.   Where?

LENNOX.   Here, my good lord.
What is't that moves your Highness?

MACBETH.   Which of you have done this?°

LORDS.   What, my good lord?   60

MACBETH.   Thou canst not say I did it. Never shake
Thy gory locks at me.°

ROSS.   Gentlemen, rise. His Highness is not well.

LADY.   Sit, worthy friends. My lord is often thus,
And hath been from his youth. Pray you keep seat.   65
The fit is momentary; upon a thought°

---

41 **From thence** elsewhere
41 **meat** food
42 **Meeting** (with a pun on "meat" in 41)
42 **bare** barren
43 **remembrancer** i.e. reminder (in the sense of one who reminds, with perhaps a playful reference to the Remembrancers who were Elizabethan court officials)
44 **wait on** attend
47 **had we** we would have
47 **honor** nobility
47 **roofed** under one roof
48 **graced** (Banquo's honors and his personal graciousness, both of which would "grace" the entertainment)

49-50 **Who . . . mischance** whom I hope I am to reprove for his unkindness in not coming tonight rather than pity for some real misfortune which has kept him away
52 **Lays . . . upon** shows some fault in
55 **Here . . . sir** Lennox presumably motions toward the chair mentioned at 11
59 **done this** (1) killed Banquo (see 61-62) (?) (2) set up this horrible practical joke (?)
61-62 **Thou . . . me** (here he addresses the figure of the dead man, who is visible to us but invisible to all others on stage)
66 **upon a thought** as quick as thought, i.e. in a moment

He will again be well. If much you note° him
You shall offend him and extend his passion.
Feed,° and regard him not.—Are you a man?

MACBETH.   Ay, and a bold one, that dare look on that   70
Which might appal the devil.

LADY.   O proper stuff!°
This is the very painting of your fear.
This is the air-drawn° dagger which you said
Led you to Duncan. O, these flaws° and starts   75
(Imposters to° true fear) would well become
A woman's story at a winter's fire,
Authorized by° her grandam. Shame itself!°
Why do you make such faces? When all's done,
You look but on a stool.°   80

MACBETH.   Prithee see there!
Behold! Look! Lo!—How say you?
Why, what care I? If thou canst nod, speak too.
If charnel houses° and our graves must send
Those that we bury back, our monuments   85
Shall be the maws° of kites.°   [*Exit Ghost.*]

LADY.   What, quite unmanned in folly?

MACBETH.   If I stand here, I saw him.

LADY.   Fie, for shame!

MACBETH.   Blood hath been shed ere now, i' th' olden time,   90
Ere humane statute° purged the gentle weal;°
Ay, and since too, murders have been performed
Too terrible for the ear. The times has° been
That, when the brains were out, the man would die,
And there an end. But now they rise again,   95

---

67 note observe and overhear
69 Feed eat
72 stuff nonsense
74 air-drawn (1) delineated by the air (2) drawn through or by the air
75 flaws outbursts
76 to compared with
78 Authorized by authenticated only by (pronounced authórized)
78 Shame itself i.e. for shame (that a man should show such unmanly terror)
80 stool (the normal seat in Shakespeare's day, especially at table)

84 charnel houses storehouses for old bones turned up when digging new graves
86 maws bellies
82-86 Lo . . . kites (Macbeth here addresses the ghost directly, as at 61-62)
85-86 our . . . kites we shall have to bury our dead by throwing them to birds of prey —*then* they won't come back
91 humane statute i.e. law
91 purged . . . weal i.e. purified the commonweal of barbarism so as to make it gentle (civilized)
93 has have

With twenty mortal murders° on their crowns,°
And push us from our stools. This is more strange
Than such a murder is.

LADY.   My worthy lord,
Your noble friends do lack° you.   100

MACBETH.   I do forget.
Do not muse° at me, my most worthy friends:
I have a strange infirmity, which is nothing
To those that know me. Come, love and health to all!
Then I'll sit down. Give me some wine, fill full.   105

Enter Ghost.

I drink to th' general joy o' th' whole table,
And to our dear friend Banquo, whom we miss.
Would he were here! To all, and him, we thirst,°
And all to all.°

LORDS.   Our duties, and the pledge.°   110

MACBETH.   Avaunt, and quit my sight! Let the earth hide thee!
Thy bones are marrowless, thy blood is cold;
Thou hast no speculation° in those eyes
Which thou dost glare with!

LADY.   Think of this, good peers,   115
But as a thing of custom. 'Tis no other.
Only° it spoils the pleasure of the time.°

MACBETH.   What man dare, I dare.
Approach thou like the rugged Russian bear,
The armed rhinoceros, or th' Hyrcan° tiger;   120
Take any shape but that,° and my firm nerves
Shall never tremble. Or be alive again
And dare me to the desert with thy sword.
If trembling I inhabit° then, protest° me

---

96 **twenty . . . murders** (see 30)
96 **crowns** heads
100 **lack** miss
102 **muse** wonder
108 **thirst** wish to drink
109 **And . . . all** everyone to everyone else
110 **Our . . . pledge** our homage to you and our toast to all
113 **speculation** comprehension

116-17 **a thing . . . Only** a customary thing—nothing more—not to be worried about except that
117 **time** i.e. the present moment
120 **Hyrcan** Hyrcania, an ancient region near the Caspian Sea, supposed to be the home of savage tigers
121 **that** i.e. that of a ghost
124 **If . . . inhabit** if I tremble
124 **protest** proclaim

The baby of a girl.° Hence, horrible shadow!   125
Unreal mock'ry, hence!   [*Exit Ghost.*]
Why, so; being gone,
I am a man again. Pray you sit still.°

LADY.   You have displaced the mirth,
Broke the good meeting with most admired° disorder.   130

MACBETH.   Can such things be,
And overcome us° like a summer's cloud
Without our special wonder? You make me strange
Even to the disposition that I owe,°
When now I think you can behold such sights   135
And keep the natural ruby of your cheeks
When mine is blanched° with fear.

Ross.   What sights, my lord?

LADY.   I pray you speak not: he grows worse and worse;
Question° enrages him. At once, good night.   140
Stand not upon the order of your going,°
But go at once.

LENNOX.   Good night and better health
Attend his Majesty.

LADY.   A kind good night to all.   *Exeunt Lords.* 145

MACBETH.   It will have blood, they say:
Blood will have blood.
Stones° have been known to move and trees° to speak;
Augures° and understood relations° have
By maggot-pies° and choughs° and rooks brought forth   150
The secret'st man of blood.° What is the night?°

LADY.   Almost at odds° with morning, which is which.

---

125 The . . . girl a baby girl (like "that
fool of a boy," etc.)
128 sit still (the guests are by this point
hurrying from the table)
130 admired wondered at
132 overcome us come over us
133-34 strange . . . owe feel unfamiliar
with my own nature
137 blanched made pale
140 Question talk
141 Stand . . . going don't wait to leave
according to rank
148 Stones i.e. stones concealing murdered corpses
148 trees i.e. probably persons transformed
to trees to silence them from revealing a
murder
149 Augures auguries, forecasts made from
such signs as the flight of birds
149 understood relations i.e. the secret
ties that relate things and events for one
who understands them
150 maggot-pies magpies
150 choughs a kind of crow which, like
the other two birds mentioned in this line,
makes a human-like utterance
150-51 brought . . . blood revealed the
identity of the most circumspect killer
151 What . . . night? How late is it?
152 at odds contesting

MACBETH.   How say'st thou,° that Macduff denies his person
    At our great bidding?

LADY.   Did you send to him, sir?   155

MACBETH.   I hear it by the way;° but I will send.
    There's not a one of them but in his house
    I keep a servant fee'd.° I will to-morrow
    (And betimes° I will) to the weyard sisters.
    More shall they speak, for now I am bent to know   160
    By the worst means the worst. For mine own good
    All causes° shall give way. I am in blood
    Stepped in so far that, should I wade no more,
    Returning were as tedious as go o'er.
    Strange things I have in head, that will to hand,   165
    Which must be acted ere they may be scanned.°

LADY.   You lack the season° of all natures, sleep.

MACBETH.   Come, we'll to sleep. My strange and self-abuse°
    Is the initiate fear° that wants hard use.
    We are yet but young in deed.   *Exeunt.* 170

                        ᴄᴏ⌒ᴏ⌒ᴏ

       Thunder. Enter the three Witches, meeting Hecate.   III v

I. WITCH.   Why, how now, Hecate? You look angerly.°

HECATE.   Have I not reason, beldams° as you are,
    Saucy and overbold? How did you dare
    To trade and traffic with Macbeth
    In riddles and affairs of death;
    And I, the mistress of your charms,   5
    The close° contriver of all harms,
    Was never called to bear my part
    Or show the glory of our art?

---

153 How . . . thou what do you think of the fact that
156 by the way incidentally
158 fee'd paid for spying
159 betimes early
162 causes considerations
166 Which . . . scanned i.e. they must be acted first, thought about only afterward

167 season preservative
168 self-abuse i.e. self-made delusion about Banquo's ghost
169 initiate fear fear of a novice (in crime)
III v 1ff see *Textual Note*
2 beldams hags
7 close secret

And, which is worse, all you have done   10
Hath been but for a wayward son,°
Spiteful and wrathful, who, as others do,
Loves for his own ends, not for you.
But make amends now: get you gone
And at the pit of Acheron°   15
Meet me i' th' morning. Thither he
Will come to know his destiny.
Your vessels and your spells provide,
Your charms and everything beside.
I am for th' air. This night I'll spend   20
Unto a dismal and a fatal end.
Great business must be wrought ere noon.
Upon the corner of the moon
There hangs a vap'rous drop profound;°
I'll catch it ere it come to ground: 25
And that, distilled by magic sleights,°
Shall raise such artificial sprites°
As by the strength of their illusion
Shall draw him on to his confusion.°
He shall spurn fate, scorn death, and bear   30
His hopes 'bove wisdom, grace, and fear:
And you all know security
Is mortals' chiefest enemy.

Music, and a song.

Hark! I am called. My little spirit,° see,
Sits in a foggy cloud and stays for me.   [*Exit.*] 35

Sing within, "Come away, come away," &c.

1. WITCH.   Come, let's make haste: she'll soon be
Back again.   *Exeunt.*

---

11 son (evidently Macbeth, but the jauntiness of tone and the references to Macbeth as spiteful, wrathful, and apparently grudging of glory to the witches (12-13) are among many elements that show this scene to be spurious—see *Textual Note*)
15 Acheron river in Hades
24 profound heavy

26 sleights skills
27 artificial sprites spirits created by magic
29 confusion ruin
34 My . . . spirit (evidently some sort of boy-coachman who descends in a car swathed in a cloud (of netting?) and then ascends with Hecate behind him)

Enter Lennox and another Lord.

LENNOX.   My former speeches
  Have but hit° your thoughts,
  Which can interpret° farther. Only I say
  Things have been strangely borne.° The gracious Duncan
  Was pitied of Macbeth. Marry,° he was dead!
  And the right valiant Banquo walked too late;
  Whom, you may say (if't please you) Fleance killed,
  For Fleance fled. Men must not walk too late.
  Who cannot want° the thought how monstrous
  It was for Malcolm and for Donalbain   10
  To kill their gracious father? Damned fact,°
  How it did grieve Macbeth! Did he not straight,°
  In pious rage, the two delinquents tear
  That were the slaves of drink and thralls° of sleep?
  Was not that nobly done? Ay, and wisely too,   15
  For 'twould have angered any heart alive
  To hear the men deny't. So that I say
  He has borne° all things well; and I do think
  That, had he Duncan's sons under his key
  (As, an't° please heaven, he shall not), they should find 20
  What 'twere to kill a father. So should Fleance.
  But peace! for from broad° words, and 'cause he failed
  His presence° at the tyrant's feast, I hear
  Macduff lives in disgrace. Sir, can you tell
  Where he bestows himself?   25

LORD.   The son of Duncan,
  From whom this tyrant holds° the due of birth,°
  Lives in the English court, and is received
  Of the most pious Edward° with such grace
  That the malevolence of fortune nothing   30
  Takes from his high respect.° Thither Macduff
  Is gone to pray the holy King upon his aid°

III vi 2 **hit** expressed
3 **interpret** i.e. guess at what I haven't
said
4 **borne** managed
5 **Marry** Mary; i.e. the Virgin Mary; an
expression of mild surprise
9 **cannot want** can avoid
11 **fact** crime
12 **straight** straightway
14 **thralls** slaves

18 **borne** handled
20 **an't** if it
22 **broad** outspoken
22-23 **failed . . . presence** failed to be
present
27 **holds** withholds
27 **due of birth** birthright, i.e. the throne
29 **Edward** Edward the Confessor (1042-66)
31 **respect** i.e. respect in which he is held
32 **upon his aid** in his behalf

..mberland and warlike Siward;°
..f these (with Him above

..we may again   35

..at, sleep to our nights,

..asts and banquets bloody knives,

..omage and receive free° honors—

..i we pine for now. And this report°

..i so exasperate° the King that he   40

..repares for some attempt of war.

LENNOX.   Sent he to Macduff?

LORD.   He did; and with an absolute "Sir, not I,"°
The cloudy° messenger turns me° his back
And hums, as who should say, "You'll rue the time   45
That clogs me with this answer."

LENNOX.   And that well might
Advise him to a caution t' hold what distance
His wisdom can provide.° Some° holy angel
Fly to the court of England and unfold   50
His message° ere he come, that a swift blessing
May soon return to this our suffering country
Under a hand accursed!

LORD.   I'll send my prayers with him.   *Exeunt.*

Thunder. Enter the three Witches.   IV i

1. WITCH.   Thrice the brinded° cat hath mewed.

2. WITCH.   Thrice, and once the hedge-pig° whined.

---

33 **Siward** Earl of Northumberland
37 **Free** i.e. remove
38 **free** freely held, not at the price of servility
39 **report** i.e. of how sympathetically Malcolm is received at the English court
40 **exasperate** exasperated
43 **"Sir, not I"** Macduff's reply
44 **cloudy** displeased
44 **turns me** turns
46 **clogs** i.e. the messenger will return reluctantly, knowing he is likely to suffer for bringing such news

48-49 **t' hold . . . provide** i.e. to flee Scotland (as he has done)
49 **Some** may some
51 **His message** (see 31ff)
IV i 1 **brinded** brindled, i.e. striped
2 **hedge-pig** hedgehog (a small hedge-haunting hog-nosed animal with erectile spines)

3. WITCH.   Harpier° cries.—'Tis time, 'tis time!

1. WITCH.   Round about the cauldron go;
    In the poisoned entrails throw.   5
    Toad, that under cold stone
    Days and nights has thirty-one
    Swelt'red° venom, sleeping got,°
    Boil thou first i' th' charmèd pot.

ALL. Double, double, toil and trouble,°   10
    Fire burn, and cauldron bubble.

2. WITCH.   Fillet° of a fenny° snake,
    In the cauldron boil and bake;
    Eye of newt,° and toe of frog,
    Wool° of bat, and tongue of dog,   15
    Adder's fork,° and blindworm's° sting
    Lizard's leg, and howlet's° wing—
    For a charm of pow'rful trouble
    Like a hell-broth boil and bubble.

ALL. Double, double, toil and trouble,   20
    Fire burn, and cauldron bubble.

3. WITCH.   Scale of dragon, tooth of wolf,
    Witch's mummy,° maw and gulf°
    Of the ravined° salt-sea shark,
    Root of hemlock° digged i' th' dark,°   25
    Liver of blaspheming Jew,
    Gall of goat, and slips of yew°
    Slivered in the moon's eclipse,°
    Nose of Turk, and Tartar's° lips,
    Finger of birth-strangled babe   30

---

3 Harpier a companion demon, like the cat and hedge-pig (see I i 9-10)
8 Swelt'red exuded
6-8 Toad . . . got i.e. a toad that has been sweating venom under a cold stone for 31 days, captured asleep (toads do in fact secrete a bitter and mildly poisonous substance on their skins)
10 Double . . . trouble the incantation aims to multiply ("double") the mischievous power that will inhere in the brew
12 Fillet slice
12 fenny swamp
14 newt water lizard
15 Wool i.e. down, soft underfeathers
16 fork i.e. cleft tongue
16 blindworm a snake-like lizard (incorrectly thought to be blind)

17 howlet owlet
23 mummy mummified flesh
23 maw and gulf stomach
24 ravined (1) ravenous with hunger (?) (2) glutted with flesh (?)
25 hemlock see note I iii 88
25 digged . . . dark i.e. at the time of its greatest potency
27 yew a tree common in English burying grounds, also reputed to be poisonous
28 eclipse i.e. the dark of the moon, always reckoned a time of ill omen
29 Turk, Tartar (probably selected for supposed cruelty and, like the Jew (26) and the babe (30), for being "unholy," i.e. outside the Christian dispensation)

Ditch-delivered° by a drab°
Make the gruel thick and slab.°
Add thereto a tiger's chaudron°
For th' ingredience° of our cauldron.

ALL.   Double, double, toil and trouble,   35
Fire burn, and cauldron bubble.

2. WITCH.   Cool it with a baboon's blood,
Then the charm is firm and good.

Enter Hecate and the other three Witches.

HECATE.   O, well done! I commend your pains,
And every one shall share i' th' gains.   40
And now about the cauldron sing
Like elves and fairies in a ring,
Enchanting all that you put in.°

Music and a song, 'Black spirits,' &c.

[*Exeunt Hecate and singers.*]

2. WITCH.   By the pricking of my thumbs,
Something wicked this way comes.   45
Open locks, whoever knocks!

Enter Macbeth.

MACBETH.   How now, you secret, black, and midnight hags,°
What is't you do?

ALL.   A deed without a name.°

MACBETH.   I conjure you by that which you profess,°   50
Howe'er you come to know it, answer me.
Though you untie the winds and let them fight
Against the churches,° though the yesty° waves
Confound and swallow navigation up,
Though bladed corn be lodged° and trees blown down,   55
Though castles topple on their warders'° heads,
Though palaces and pyramids do slope

---

31 **Ditch-delivered** ditch-born
31 **drab** whore
32 **slab** slimy
33 **chaudron** entrails
34 **ingredience** see note I vii 11
39-43 **O, well . . . in** see *Textual Note*
47 **secret . . . hags** Macbeth addresses
them as representatives of black magic
49 **without a name** too unholy to be identified

50 **that . . . profess** i.e. your magic art
52-53 **Though . . . churches** see note I
iii 12
53 **yesty** yeasty, i.e. foamy
55 **Though . . . lodged** though wheat in
the blade (i.e. before the grain is formed)
be beaten down and thus the crop ruined
56 **warders'** keepers'

Their heads to their foundations, though the treasure
Of nature's germens° tumble all together
Even till destruction sicken, answer me   60
To what I ask you.°

1. WITCH.   Speak.

2. WITCH.   Demand.

3. WITCH.   We'll answer.

1. WITCH.   Say if th' hadst rather hear it from our mouths   65
Or from our masters.

MACBETH.   Call 'em. Let me see 'em.

1. WITCH.   Pour in sow's blood, that hath eaten
Her nine farrow,° grease that's sweaten°
From the murderer's gibbet throw   70
Into the flame.

ALL.   Come, high or low,
Thyself and office° deftly show!

Thunder. First Apparition, an Armed Head.

MACBETH.   Tell me, thou unknown power—

1. WITCH.   He knows thy thought: 75
Hear his speech, but say thou naught.

1. APPARITION.   Macbeth, Macbeth, Macbeth,
Beware Macduff!
Beware the Thane of Fife! Dismiss me.—Enough.

He descends.

MACBETH.   Whate'er thou art, for thy good caution thanks: 80
Thou hast harped° my fear aright. But one word more—

---

59 nature's germens i.e. the "seeds" (I
iii 60-61) from which, as they germinate in
the fullness of time, all things in the universe are brought to pass (Macbeth in effect
says: even if you have to destroy the whole
universe to do it, answer me)
52-61 Though . . . you (Macbeth mani-
fests his right to diabolical aid by the character of his conjuration, which is willing to
accept the ruin of churches, commerce, har-
vests, dwellings, tombs, and even nature
itself)
69 farrow piglets
69 sweaten sweated
72 high or low i.e. from upper air or inner earth

73 office function
73 s.d. Armed Head (variously thought to
allude to (1) Macduff, the warrior Macbeth
must yet fear (2) Macbeth's own severed
head, with which Macduff enters at the end
of the play (3) rebellious violence generally—with which Macbeth has been associated
ever since the bloody sergeant's first description of him in battle, I ii 18-25 and
60-63. Duncan gave him the title of the
rebel Thane of Cawdor, which presumably
is to die with him)
79 s.d. descends i.e. through a trap door
81 harped guessed

1. WITCH.   He will not be commanded. Here's another,
More potent than the first.

Thunder. Second Apparition, a Bloody Child.°

2. APPARITION.   Macbeth, Macbeth, Macbeth—

MACBETH.   Had I three ears, I'ld hear thee.   85

2. APPARITION.   Be bloody, bold, and resolute!
Laugh to scorn
The pow'r of man, for none of woman born
Shall harm Macbeth.   *Descends.*

MACBETH.   Then live, Macduff,—what need I fear of thee?   90
But yet I'll make assurance double sure
And take a bond° of fate. Thou shalt not live;
That I may tell pale-hearted fear it lies°
And sleep in spite of thunder.

Thunder. Third Apparition, a Child Crowned,
with a tree in his hand.°

What is this that rises like the issue° of a king   95
And wears upon his baby-brow the round
And top° of sovereignty?

ALL.   Listen, but speak not to't.

3. APPARITION.   Be lion-mettled, proud, and take no care
Who chafes, who frets, or where conspirers are!   100
Macbeth shall never vanquished be until
Great Birnam Wood to high Dunsinane Hill
Shall come against him.   *Descends.*

MACBETH.   That will never be.
Who can impress° the forest, bid the tree   105
Unfix his earth-bound root?° Sweet bodements,° good!

---

83 s.d. **Bloody Child** (generally accepted
as a reference to (1) Macduff [see V viii
19-20] and (2) life's capacity to produce,
through pain and struggle, creative forces
that drive out destructive ones, as Macduff
does for Scotland at the cost of his wife
and children; the fact that this apparition
is "More potent" than the first possibly
suggests, therefore, that the second and
third interpretations of the first apparition
[see note 73 s.d.] have the best foundation)
92 **bond** guarantee
93 **lies** i.e. in telling me I am in danger
94 s.d. **Child Crowned . . . hand** (in view
of Malcolm's strategem [V iv 6-9, v 34-40,

and vi 1-3] and his crowning, this apparition may plausibly refer to him specifically,
and, more generally, to the triumphant inheritance that may wait for mankind in
those unfolding processes of birth and
growth and time that are to make Malcolm
king and Banquo's descendants kings)
95 **issue** offspring
96-97 **round And top** crown
105 **impress** conscript
105-6 **Who . . . root?** (Macbeth forgets his
own earlier knowledge [III iv 148] that trees
may even *speak* to convict a murderer)
106 **bodements** prophecies

Rebellious dead rise never till the Wood
Of Birnam rise, and our high-placed Macbeth
Shall live the lease of nature,° pay his breath
To time and mortal custom.° Yet my heart   110
Throbs to know one thing. Tell me, if your art
Can tell so much: Shall Banquo's issue ever
Reign in this kingdom?

ALL.   Seek to know no more.

MACBETH.   I will be satisfied. Deny me this,   115
And an eternal curse fall on you! Let me know.
Why sinks° that cauldron? and what noise is this?

                               Hautboys.

1. WITCH.   Show!

2. WITCH.   Show!

3. WITCH.   Show!   120

ALL.   Show his eyes, and grieve his heart!
Come like shadows, so depart!

         A show° of eight Kings and Banquo,
         last [King] with a glass in his hand.

MACBETH.   Thou art too like the spirit of Banquo. Down!
Thy crown does sear mine eyeballs. And thy hair,°
Thou other gold-bound brow, is like the first.   125
A third is like the former. Filthy hags,
Why do you show me this? A fourth? Start, eyes!
What, will the line stretch out to th' crack of doom?
Another yet? A seventh? I'll see no more.
And yet the eighth appears, who bears a glass°   130
Which shows me many more; and some I see
That twofold balls and treble sceptres° carry.
Horrible sight! Now I see 'tis true;
For the blood-boltered° Banquo smiles upon me
And points at them for his. What? Is this so?   135

---

109 lease of nature average lifespan
110 mortal custom natural death
117 sinks (again, through one of the trap doors)
122 s.d. show (since Macbeth sees them successively, this "show" is evidently a procession)
124 hair general appearance
130 glass magic mirror showing the future

132 twofold . . . sceptres coronation insignia (the ball is the royal orb carried in the left hand, here double since the Stuarts held both England and Scotland; the sceptres are treble because two were used in English coronations and one in Scottish)
134 blood-boltered i.e. his hair is matted with blood

1. WITCH.   Ay, sir, all this is so. But why
    Stands Macbeth thus amazedly?
    Come, sisters, cheer we up his sprites°
    And show the best of our delights.
    I'll charm the air to give a sound   140
    While you perform your antic° round,°
    That this great king may kindly say
    Our duties did his welcome pay.°

          Music. The Witches dance, and vanish.

MACBETH.   Where are they? Gone?
    Let this pernicious hour   145
    Stand aye accursèd in the calendar!
    Come in, without there!

          Enter Lennox.

LENNOX.   What's your Grace's will?

MACBETH.   Saw you the weyard sisters?

LENNOX.   No, my lord.   150

MACBETH.   Came they not by you?

LENNOX.   No indeed, my lord.

MACBETH.   Infected be the air whereon they ride,
    And damned° all those that trust them! I did hear
    The galloping of horse. Who was't came by?   155

LENNOX.   'Tis two or three, my lord, that bring you word
    Macduff is fled to England.

MACBETH.   Fled to England?

LENNOX.   Ay, my good lord.

MACBETH.   [*aside*] Time, thou anticipat'st my dread exploits.   160
    The flighty purpose never is o'ertook
    Unless the deed go with it.° From this moment
    The very firstlings° of my heart shall be
    The firstlings of my hand. And even now,
    To crown my thoughts with acts, be it thought and done: 165
    The castle of Macduff I will surprise,

---

138 **sprites** spirits
141 **antic** grotesque
141 **round** circular dance
136-43 **Ay, sir . . . pay** see *Textual Note*
154 **damned** (a fate thus wished on himself)

161-62 **The flighty . . . it** i.e. our fleeting purpose is never fulfilled ("o'ertook") unless our execution of that purpose ("the deed") is so swift as to accompany it ("go with it")
163 **firstlings** firstborn, i.e. first thoughts

Seize upon Fife, give to the edge o' th' sword
His wife, his babes, and all unfortunate souls
That trace° him in his line. No boasting like a fool;
This deed I'll do before this purpose cool.   170
But no more sights!—Where are these gentlemen?
Come, bring me where they are.   *Exeunt.*

Enter Macduff's Wife, her Son, and Ross.   IV ii

WIFE.   What had he done to make him fly the land?

ROSS.   You must have patience, madam.

WIFE.   He had none.
His flight was madness. When our actions do not,
Our fears do make us traitors.°   5

ROSS.   You know not
Whether it was his wisdom or his fear.

WIFE.   Wisdom? To leave his wife, to leave his babes,
His mansion and his titles° in a place
From whence himself does fly? He loves us not,   10
He wants° the natural touch.° For the poor wren
(The most diminutive of birds) will fight,
Her young ones in her nest,° against the owl.
All is the fear and nothing is the love,
As little is the wisdom, where the flight   15
So runs against all reason.

ROSS.   My dearest coz,°
I pray you school° yourself. But for your husband,
He is noble, wise, judicious, and best knows
The fits° o' th' season. I dare not speak much further,   20

---

169 trace track, i.e. follow in his blood line
IV ii 5 Our . . . traitors i.e. the flight to which he was led by his fears (for Scotland? for himself?) will be called treason by Macbeth
9 titles possessions
11 wants lacks
11 natural touch i.e. natural affection
13 Her . . . nest when she has young in her nest
17 coz kinswoman ("coz" is short for "cousin")
18 school control
20 fits disorders

But cruel are the times when we are traitors
And do not know ourselves; when we hold rumor
From what we fear, yet know not what we fear
But float upon a wild and violent sea
Each way and none.° I take my leave of you.   25
Shall not be long but I'll be here again.
Things at the worst will cease,° or else climb upward
To what they were before.—My pretty cousin,
Blessing upon you!

WIFE.   Fathered he is,   30
And yet he's fatherless.

ROSS.   I am so much a fool, should I stay longer
It would be my disgrace° and your discomfort.
I take my leave at once.   *Exit.*

WIFE.   Sirrah,° your father's dead;   35
And what will you do now? How will you live?

SON.   As birds do, mother.

WIFE.   What, with worms and flies?

SON.   With what I get, I mean; and so do they.

WIFE.   Poor bird!   40
Thou'dst never fear the net nor lime,°
The pitfall° nor the gin.°

SON.   Why should I, mother?
Poor birds° they are not set for.
My father is not dead for all your saying.   45

WIFE.   Yes, he is dead.
How wilt thou do for a father?

SON.   Nay, how will you do for a husband?

WIFE.   Why, I can buy me twenty at any market.

SON.   Then you'll buy 'em to sell again.   50

21-25 when . . . none when we can be made traitors (because the powers that be say so) without knowing we are; when we can be made fearful by rumors without knowing precisely what we fear, fluctuating this way and that as on a wild **sea**
27 cease (this probably means "cease worsening," but it may instead imply "cease to matter" because one is either unconscious or dead—see *King Lear* IV i 1-30)

33 disgrace i.e. he would begin to weep
35 Sirrah term of address used to menials and children
41 lime birdlime, gluey substance spread on branches to catch birds
42 pitfall trap with a door that falls to prevent escape
42 gin engine, i.e. any device for snaring
44 Poor birds i.e. birds (like himself—see 40) from whose death nothing is gained

WIFE. Thou speak'st with all thy wit;
       And yet, i' faith, with wit enough for thee.°

SON. Was my father a traitor, mother?

WIFE. Ay, that he was!

SON. What is a traitor?   55

WIFE. Why, one that swears and lies.°

SON. And be all traitors that do so?

WIFE. Every one that does so is a traitor
       And must be hanged.

SON. And must they all be hanged that swear and lie?   60

WIFE. Every one.

SON. Who must hang them?

WIFE. Why, the honest men.

SON. Then the liars and swearers are fools, for there are liars
      and swearers enow° to beat the honest men and hang up   65
      them.

WIFE. Now God help thee, poor monkey!
       But how wilt thou do for a father?

SON. If he were dead, you'ld weep for him. If you would not,
      it were a good sign that I should quickly have a new   70
      father.

WIFE. Poor prattler, how thou talk'st!

                    Enter a Messenger.

MESSENGER. Bless you, fair dame! I am not to you known,
            Though in your state of honor I am perfect.°
            I doubt° some danger does approach you nearly.   75
            If you will take a homely° man's advice,
            Be not found here. Hence with your little ones!
            To fright you thus methinks I am too savage;
            To do worse to you° were fell° cruelty,
            Which is too nigh your person. Heaven preserve you! 80
            I dare abide no longer.   *Exit.*

51-52 **with all . . . thee** i.e. with a child's
limited view, and yet what you say is not
bad, for a child
56 **swears and lies** i.e. swears oaths and
breaks them (as she feels her husband has
done in fleeing the country)
65 **enow** enough

74 **in your . . . perfect** perfectly familiar
with your rank and quality
75 **doubt** fear
76 **homely** humble
79 **To do . . . you** i.e. not to warn you
79 **fell** savage

WIFE.   Whither should I fly?
I have done no harm. But I remember now
I am in this earthly world, where to do harm
Is often laudable, to do good sometime   85
Accounted dangerous folly. Why then, alas,
Do I put up that womanly defense
To say I have done no harm?
What are these faces?

Enter Murderers.

MURDERER.   Where is your husband?   90

WIFE.   I hope in no place so unsanctified
Where such as thou mayst find him.

MURDERER.   He's a traitor.

SON.   Thou liest, thou shag-eared° villain!

MURDERER.   What, you egg!   [*Stabs him.*] 95
Young fry° of treachery!

SON.   He has killed me, mother.
Run away, I pray you!   [*Dies.*]
Exit [Wife], crying "Murder!" [pursued by Murderers].

⸀⸏⸎⸏⸎⸏⸎

Enter Malcolm and Macduff.   IV ⟩

MALCOLM.   Let us seek out some desolate shade, and there
Weep our sad bosoms empty.

MACDUFF.   Let us rather
Hold fast the mortal° sword and, like good men,
Bestride° our downfall'n birthdom. Each new morn   5
New widows howl, new orphans cry, new sorrows
Strike heaven on the face, that° it resounds
As if it felt with Scotland and yelled out
Like syllable of dolor.°

---

94 **shag-eared** i.e. shaggy-eared (having
long hair lapping over his ears)
96 **fry** spawn
IV iii 4 **mortal** death-dealing

5 **Bestride** i.e. to defend it (like the body
of a fallen comrade in battle)
7 **that** so that
9 **Like . . . dolor** equal cry of pain

MALCOLM.   What I believe, I'll wail;   10
    What know, believe;° and what I can redress,
    As I shall find the time to friend,° I will.
    What you have spoke, it may be so perchance.
    This tyrant, whose sole name blisters our tongues,
    Was once thought honest; you have loved him well;   15
    He hath not touched you yet.° I am young; but something
    You may discern of him through me, and wisdom
    To offer° up a weak, poor, innocent lamb
    T' appease an angry god.

MACDUFF.   I am not treacherous.   20

MALCOLM.   But Macbeth is.
    A good and virtuous nature may recoil
    In an imperial charge.° But I shall crave your pardon.
    That which you are, my thoughts cannot transpose:°
    Angels are bright still though the brightest° fell;   25
    Though all things foul would wear the brows of grace,
    Yet grace must still look so.°

MACDUFF.   I have lost my hopes.

MALCOLM.   Perchance even there°
    Where I did find my doubts.   30
    Why in that rawness° left you wife and child,
    Those precious motives, those strong knots° of love,
    Without leave-taking? I pray you,
    Let not my jealousies be your dishonors,

---

11 What . . . believe i.e. what I know
from other sources I'll believe (Malcolm is
mistrustful of Macduff, fearing he may be
Macbeth's agent)
12 to friend to be propitious
16 He . . . yet (a further reason for sup-
posing Macduff may be in Macbeth's em-
ploy, one that will be shattered in this
scene)
16-18 something . . . offer (no satisfactory
interpretation exists; the possibilities are:
(1) you may discern something of Macbeth's
nature by considering my predicament,
which is of his making, and from this you
may discern as well the wisdom of offering,
etc. (?) (2) your plan may be to discern
something of the degree of Macbeth's security by probing my intention ["discern of
him through me"] and hence discover that
it may be wisdom to offer, etc. (?) (3)
"You may see something to your advantage
by betraying me" (Upton), and thus see the

wisdom of, etc.; many editors emend the
Folio's "discerne" to *deserve*, but "wisdom" must then be understood as a subject without a verb, so that it becomes
necessary [strictly speaking] to make another
change and insert "it is" or "'tis," giving
"and it is wisdom" or "and wisdom 'tis,"
etc.)
22-23 recoil . . . charge go back on itself
when under a royal command (the meta-
phor is from cannon fire)
24 transpose alter
25 the brightest i.e. Lucifer
27 so i.e. like itself
29 there i.e. in the suspicious fact that
you left your family unprotected, which you
would hardly do if Macbeth were *really*
your enemy
31 rawness insecurity
32 knots i.e. by which, therefore, one is
necessarily tied

But mine own safeties.° You may be rightly just   35
Whatever I shall think.

MACDUFF.   Bleed, bleed, poor country!
　　　　Great tyranny, lay thou thy basis° sure,
　　　　For goodness dare not check thee, wear thou thy wrongs,
　　　　The title is affeered!° Fare thee well, lord.   40
　　　　I would not be the villain that thou think'st
　　　　For the whole space that's in the tyrant's grasp
　　　　And the rich East to boot.°

MALCOLM.   Be not offended.
　　　　I speak not as in absolute fear of you.   45
　　　　I think our country sinks beneath the yoke,
　　　　It weeps, it bleeds, and each new day a gash
　　　　Is added to her wounds. I think withal°
　　　　There would be hands uplifted in my right;
　　　　And here from gracious England° have I offer   50
　　　　Of goodly thousands. But, for all this,
　　　　When I shall tread upon the tyrant's head
　　　　Or wear it on my sword, yet my poor country
　　　　Shall have more vices than it had before,
　　　　More suffer, and more sundry ways than ever,   55
　　　　By him that shall succeed.

MACDUFF.   What should he be?

MALCOLM.   It is myself I mean, in whom I know
　　　　All the particulars° of vice so grafted°
　　　　That, when they shall be opened,° black Macbeth   60
　　　　Will seem as pure as snow, and the poor state
　　　　Esteem him as a lamb, being compared
　　　　With my confineless harms.

MACDUFF.   Not in the legions
　　　　Of horrid hell can come a devil more damned   65
　　　　In evils to top Macbeth.

MALCOLM.   I grant him bloody,
　　　　Luxurious,° avaricious, false, deceitful,

34-35 **Let . . . safeties** don't interpret my
suspicions as dishonoring you, but only as
protecting me
38 **basis** foundation
40 **affeered** legally confirmed
43 **to boot** besides
48 **withal** moreover

50 **gracious England** i.e. the King of
England, Edward the Confessor
59 **particulars** particular kinds
59 **grafted** implanted
60 **opened** i.e. like the flower buds on a
grafted tree
68 **Luxurious** lecherous

    Sudden,° malicious, smacking of every sin
    That has a name. But there's no bottom, none,   70
    In my voluptuousness. Your wives, your daughters,
    Your matrons, and your maids could not fill up
    The cistern of my lust; and my desire
    All continent° impediments would o'erbear
    That did oppose my will. Better Macbeth   75
    Than such an one to reign.

MACDUFF.   Boundless intemperance
    In nature° is a tyranny.° It hath been°
    Th' untimely emptying of the happy throne
    And fall of many kings. But fear not yet   80
    To take upon you what is yours.° You may
    Convey° your pleasures in a spacious plenty
    And yet seem cold—the time° you may so hoodwink.°
    We have willing dames enough. There cannot be
    That vulture in you tó devour so many   85
    As will to greatness dedicate themselves,
    Finding it so inclined.°

MALCOLM.   With this there grows
    In my most ill-composed affection° such
    A stanchless° avarice that, were I King,   90
    I should cut off the nobles for° their lands,
    Desire his° jewels, and this other's house,
    And my more-having would be as a sauce
    To make me hunger more, that° I should forge
    Quarrels unjust against the good and loyal,   95
    Destroying them for wealth.

MACDUFF.   This avarice
    Sticks deeper, grows with more pernicious root
    Than summer-seeming° lust, and it hath been

---

69 Sudden violent
74 continent (1) restraining (2) chaste
78 nature i.e. human nature
78 tyranny i.e. because (like a tyrant in the state) it overrules all else
78 been been the cause of
81 what is yours i.e. the throne
82 Convey manage clandestinely
83 the time the world
83 hoodwink deceive
87 Finding . . . inclined as soon as they find that greatness, i.e. the king, is lustfully inclined

89 ill-composed affection unbalanced character
90 stanchless insatiable
91 for i.e. to get
92 his i.e. one man's
94 that so that
99 summer-seeming (whether this means "summer-beseeming," i.e. suited to the summer of one's life, or "summer-resembling,"' the point is that it passes much sooner than avarice)

The sword° of our slain kings. Yet do not fear.   100
Scotland hath foisons° to fill up your will°
Of your mere own.° All these are portable,°
With other graces weighed.

MALCOLM.   But I have none. The king-becoming graces,
As justice, verity, temp'rance, stableness,   105
Bounty, perseverance, mercy, lowliness,°
Devotion, patience, courage, fortitude,
I have no relish° of them, but abound
In the division° of each several crime,
Acting it many ways. Nay, had I pow'r, I should   110
Pour the sweet milk of concord into hell,
Uproar° the universal peace, confound
All unity on earth.

MACDUFF.   O Scotland, Scotland!

MALCOLM.   If such a one be fit to govern, speak.   115
I am as I have spoken.

MACDUFF.   Fit to govern? No, not to live! O nation miserable,
With an untitled° tyrant bloody-sceptred,
When shalt thou see thy wholesome days again,
Since that the truest issue of thy throne   120
By his own interdiction° stands accursed
And does blaspheme his breed?° Thy royal father
Was a most sainted king; the queen that bore thee,
Oft'ner upon her knees than on her feet,
Died° every day she lived. Fare thee well.   125
These evils thou repeat'st upon thyself
Hath° banished me from Scotland. O my breast,
Thy hope ends here!

MALCOLM.   Macduff, this noble passion,
Child of integrity, hath from my soul   130
Wiped the black scruples,° reconciled my thoughts

---

100 **sword** i.e. the cause of death
101 **foisons** abundant resources
101 **will** desire
102 **Of . . . own** i.e. from royal holdings alone
102 **portable** supportable
106 **lowliness** humility
108 **relish** trace
109 **division** i.e. all the possible variants
112 **Uproar** blast

118 **untitled** i.e. usurping, having no title to the throne
121 **interdiction** legal statement of unfitness
122 **blaspheme . . . breed** defame the parents who bred him
125 **Died** (to the concerns of this world)
127 **Hath** have
131 **scruples** suspicions

To thy good truth and honor. Devilish Macbeth
By many of these trains° hath sought to win me
Into his power; and modest° wisdom plucks° me
From over-credulous haste; but God above   135
Deal between thee and me,° for even now
I put myself to thy direction and
Unspeak mine own detraction, here abjure
The taints and blames I laid upon myself
For° strangers to my nature. I am yet   140
Unknown to woman, never was forsworn,°
Scarcely have coveted what was mine own,
At no time broke my faith, would not betray
The devil to his fellow, and delight
No less in truth than life. My first false speaking   145
Was this upon° myself. What I am truly,
Is thine and my poor country's to command;
Whither indeed, before thy here-approach,
Old Siward with ten thousand warlike men
Already at a point° for setting forth.   150
Now we'll° together; and the chance of goodness
Be like our warranted quarrel!° Why are you silent?

MACDUFF.   Such welcome and unwelcome things at once
    'Tis hard to reconcile.

Enter a Doctor.

MALCOLM.   Well, more anon. Comes the King forth,   155
    I pray you?

DOCTOR.   Ay, sir. There are a crew of wretched souls
    That stay° his cure. Their malady convinces°
    The great assay of art;° but at his touch,
    Such sanctity hath heaven given his hand,   160
    They presently° amend.

---

133 **trains** (Shakespeare may have in mind enticements for animals made by drawing bait along the ground, or courses of gunpowder laid to set off mines under the walls of a besieged city)
134 **modest** prudent
134 **plucks** restrains
136 **Deal . . . me** judge between us
140 **For** as
141 **forsworn** perjured
146 **upon** against

150 **at a point** readied
151 **we'll** we'll go
151-52 **the chance . . . quarrel** let our chance of success be as good as our cause is just
158 **stay** wait for
158 **convinces** baffles
159 **The . . . art** the utmost application of the art of medicine
161 **presently** immediately

MALCOLM.   I thank you, doctor.   *Exit [Doctor].*

MACDUFF.   What's the disease he means?

MALCOLM.   'Tis called the evil.°
    A most miraculous work in this good King,   165
    Which often since my here-remain in England
    I have seen him do: how he solicits° heaven
    Himself best knows, but strangely-visited° people,
    All swol'n and ulcerous, pitiful to the eye,
    The mere° despair of surgery,° he cures,   170
    Hanging a golden stamp° about their necks,
    Put on with holy prayers; and 'tis spoken,°
    To the succeeding royalty he leaves
    The healing benediction. With this strange virtue,°
    He hath a heavenly gift of prophecy,   175
    And sundry blessings hang about his throne
    That speak him full of grace.

Enter Ross.

MACDUFF.   See who comes here.

MALCOLM.   My countryman; but yet I know him not.

MACDUFF.   My ever gentle cousin, welcome hither.   180

MALCOLM.   I know him now. Good God betimes° remove
    The means° that makes us strangers!

ROSS.   Sir, amen.

MACDUFF.   Stands Scotland where it did?

ROSS.   Alas, poor country,   185
    Almost afraid to know itself. It cannot
    Be called our mother but our grave, where nothing°
    But who knows nothing is once seen to smile;
    Where sighs and groans, and shrieks that rent the air,
    Are made, not marked;° where violent sorrow seems   190
    A modern ecstasy.° The dead man's knell

---

164 **evil** the King's evil, scrofula—which Edward the Confessor was the first English king to touch for
167 **solicits** influences
168 **visited** afflicted
170 **mere** utter
170 **surgery** medicine
171 **stamp** coin
172 **'tis spoken** i.e. it's said that
174 **virtue** healing power
181 **betimes** speedily
182 **means** cause, i.e. Macbeth
187 **nothing** no one
190 **marked** remarked, noted
191 **modern ecstasy** commonplace excitement

Is there scarce asked for who,° and good men's lives
Expire before the flowers in their caps,
Dying or ere they sicken.°

MACDUFF.   O, relation too nice,° and yet too true!   195

MALCOLM.   What's the newest grief?

ROSS.   That of an hour's age doth hiss° the speaker;
Each minute teems° a new one.

MACDUFF.   How does my wife?

ROSS.   Why, well.   200

MACDUFF.   And all my children?

ROSS.   Well too.

MACDUFF.   The tyrant has not battered at their peace?

ROSS.   No, they were well at peace when I did leave 'em.

MACDUFF.   Be not a niggard of your speech. How goes't?   205

ROSS.   When I came hither to transport the tidings
Which I have heavily° borne, there ran a rumor
Of many worthy fellows that were out,°
Which was to my belief witnessed the rather
For that° I saw the tyrant's power° afoot.   210
Now is the time of help. Your° eye in Scotland
Would create soldiers, make our women fight
To doff their dire distresses.

MALCOLM.   Be't their comfort
We are coming thither. Gracious England hath   215
Lent us good Siward and ten thousand men,
An older and a better soldier none
That Christendom gives out.°

ROSS.   Would I could answer
This comfort with the like. But I have words   220
That would° be howled out in the desert air,
Where hearing should not latch° them.

191-92 **The dead . . . who** no one inquires
for whom the death-bell tolls (because it
tolls so often)
194 **Dying . . . sicken** i.e. they are murdered
195 **nice** exact
197 **hiss** cause to be hissed (because his
news is already obsolete)
198 **teems** brings forth
207 **heavily** sadly

208 **out** in arms
209-10 **witnessed . . . that** supported all
the more because
210 **power** i.e. army
211 **Your** i.e. Malcolm's
217-18 **An . . . out** i.e. the whole of
Christendom knows no more experienced
or better soldier
221 **would** should
222 **latch** catch

MACDUFF.   What concern they,
    The general cause or is it a fee-grief°
    Due° to some single breast?   225

Ross.   No mind that's honest
    But in it shares some woe, though the main part
    Pertains to you alone.

MACDUFF.   If it be mine,
    Keep it not from me, quickly let me have it.   230

Ross.   Let not your ears despise my tongue for ever,
    Which shall possess them with the heaviest sound
    That ever yet they heard.

MACDUFF.   Humh! I guess at it.

Ross.   Your castle is surprised, your wife and babes   235
    Savagely slaughtered. To relate the manner
    Were, on the quarry° of these murdered deer,
    To add the death of you.

MALCOLM.   Merciful heaven!
    What, man! Ne'er pull your hat upon your brows.   240
    Give sorrow words. The grief that does not speak
    Whispers° the o'erfraught° heart and bids it break.

MACDUFF.   My children too?

Ross.   Wife, children, servants, all that could be found.

MACDUFF.   And I must be from thence? My wife killed too?   245

Ross.   I have said.

MALCOLM.   Be comforted.
    Let's make us med'cines of our great revenge°
    To cure this deadly grief.

MACDUFF.   He has no children.° All my pretty ones?   250
    Did you say all? O hell-kite! All?
    What, all my pretty chickens and their dam
    At one fell swoop?

---

224 fee-grief private sorrow (so-called by analogy with land held "legally in fee," i.e. exclusively)
225 Due belonging
237 on the quarry i.e. to the dead bodies (the quarry is the game killed during the hunt)
242 Whispers whispers to
242 o'erfraught overburdened

248 make . . . revenge i.e. heal our wounds with our plans for revenge
250 He . . . children (this may mean either that Macbeth has no children and hence that no revenge great enough can be taken on him or it may be a comment on the ingenuousness of Malcolm's idea that a father's grief can be lost in revenge)

MALCOLM.   Dispute it° like a man.

MACDUFF.   I shall do so;   255
> But I must also feel it as a man.
> I cannot but remember such things were
> That were most precious to me. Did heaven look on
> And would not take their part? Sinful Macduff,
> They were all struck for thee! Naught° that I am,   260
> Not for their own demerits but for mine
> Fell slaughter on their souls. Heaven rest them now!

MALCOLM.   Be this the whetstone of your sword. Let grief
> Convert to anger; blunt not the heart, enrage it.

MACDUFF.   O, I could play the woman with mine eyes   265
> And braggart with my tongue.° But, gentle heavens,
> Cut short all intermission.° Front° to front
> Bring thou this fiend of Scotland and myself.
> Within my sword's length set him. If he scape,°
> Heaven forgive him too!   270

MALCOLM.   This tune goes manly.
> Come, go we to the King. Our power is ready;
> Our lack is nothing but our leave.° Macbeth
> Is ripe for shaking,° and the pow'rs above
> Put on their instruments.° Receive what cheer you may.   275
> The night is long that never finds the day.   *Exeunt.*

∽◦◦∽⁌∽◦◦∽

Enter a Doctor of Physic and a Waiting Gentlewoman.   V i

DOCTOR.   I have two nights watched with you, but can perceive
no truth in your report. When was it she last walked?

---

254 **Dispute it** fight back
260 **Naught** wicked
265-66 **O . . . tongue** i.e. unmanly tears of
grief mix with a manly desire to boast
about the revenge he will take
267 **intermission** delay
267 **Front** forehead, i.e. face

269 **scape** escape
273 **Our . . . leave** all we lack is taking
leave
274 **shaking** i.e. like a tree of ripe fruit
275 **Put . . . instruments** (1) arm themselves (?) (2) urge us, their agents, onward
(?)

GENTLEWOMAN.   Since his Majesty went into the field° I have
      seen her rise from her bed, throw her nightgown° upon
      her, unlock her closet,° take forth paper, fold it, write 5
      upon't, read it, afterwards seal it, and again return to bed;
      yet all this while in a most fast sleep.

DOCTOR.   A great perturbation in nature, to receive at once the
      benefit of sleep and do the effects of watching!° In this
      slumb'ry agitation, besides her walking and other actual° 10
      performances, what (at any time) have you heard her say?

GENTLEWOMAN.   That, sir, which I will not report after her.

DOCTOR.   You may to me, and 'tis most meet° you should.

GENTLEWOMAN.   Neither to you nor any one, having no witness
      to confirm my speech.   15

          Enter Lady [Macbeth], with a taper.

      Lo you, here she comes! This is her very guise,° and, upon
      my life, fast asleep! Observe her; stand close.

DOCTOR.   How came she by that light?

GENTLEWOMAN.   Why, it stood by her. She has light by her
      continually. 'Tis her command.   20

DOCTOR.   You see her eyes are open.

GENTLEWOMAN.   Ay, but their sense are° shut.

DOCTOR.   What is it she does now?
      Look how she rubs her hands.

GENTLEWOMAN.   It is an accustomed action with her, to seem 25
      thus washing her hands. I have known her continue in
      this a quarter of an hour.

LADY.   Yet here's a spot.

DOCTOR.   Hark, she speaks. I will set down what comes from
      her, to satisfy my remembrance the more strongly.   30

V i 3 went . . . field (with his army to
put down rebellion)
4 nightgown dressing gown
5 closet chest
9 watching waking
10 actual i.e. taking the form of action
13 meet fitting
16 guise custom
22 are (though the actual subject is singular, the idea of two unseeing eyes has
been evoked by use of a plural verb)

LADY. Out, damnèd spot! Out, I say! One—two°—why then 'tis time to do't. Hell is murky. Fie, my lord, fie! a soldier and afeard? What need we fear who knows it, when none can call our pow'r to accompt?° Yet who would have thought the old man to have had so much blood in him? 35

DOCTOR. Do you mark that?

LADY. The Thane of Fife had a wife. Where is she now? What, will these hands ne'er be clean? No more o' that, my lord, no more o' that! You mar all with this starting.°

DOCTOR. Go to, go to! 40
You° have known what you should not.

GENTLEWOMAN. She has spoke what she should not, I am sure of that. Heaven knows what she has known.

LADY. Here's the smell of the blood still. All the perfumes of Arabia will not sweeten this little hand. Oh, oh, oh! 45

DOCTOR. What a sigh is there! The heart is sorely charged.°

GENTLEWOMAN. I would not have such a heart in my bosom for the dignity of the whole body.°

DOCTOR. Well, well, well.

GENTLEWOMAN. Pray God it be,° sir. 50

DOCTOR. This disease is beyond my practice.° Yet I have known those which have walked in their sleep who have died holily in their beds.

LADY. Wash your hands, put on your nightgown, look not so pale! I tell you yet again, Banquo's buried. He cannot come out on's° grave. 55

DOCTOR. Even so?

LADY. To bed, to bed! There's knocking at the gate. Come, come, come, come, give me your hand! What's done cannot be undone.° To bed, to bed, to bed! *Exit.* 60

31 **One—two** (perpetually reliving the night of Duncan's murder, Lady Macbeth recalls its events [and other horrors, like the return of Banquo and the slaughter of Macduff's family] not in any orderly sequence but in chaotic flashes; here she apparently hears the clock strike two, which must have been the hour of the deed)
34 **accompt** account
39 **starting** startled behavior (see III iv 75)
41 **You** Lady Macbeth
46 **charged** burdened

48 **for . . . body** (1) though I were to be rewarded for having it with the value of the *whole* body (?) (2) even if having it were to give me the rank (dignity) that she has, i.e. make me a queen (?)
50 **it be** i.e. it be well (she takes his expletive "well" as an adjective)
51 **practice** skill
56 **out on's** out of his
59-60 **What's . . . undone** see I vii 1 and III ii 14

DOCTOR.   Will she go now to bed?

GENTLEWOMAN.   Directly.

DOCTOR.   Foul whisp'rings are abroad. Unnatural deeds
  Do breed unnatural troubles. Infected° minds
  To their deaf pillows will discharge their secrets.   65
  More needs she the divine° than the physician.
  God, God forgive us all! Look after her;
  Remove from her the means of all annoyance,°
  And still° keep eyes upon her. So good night.
  My mind she has mated,° and amazed my sight.   70
  I think, but dare not speak.

GENTLEWOMAN.   Good night, good doctor.   *Exeunt.*

Drum and Colors. Enter Menteith, Caithness, V ii
Angus, Lennox, Soldiers.

MENTEITH.   The English pow'r° is near, led on by Malcolm,
  His uncle Siward, and the good Macduff.
  Revenges burn in them; for their dear° causes°
  Would to the bleeding° and the grim alarm°
  Excite the mortified° man.   5

ANGUS.   Near Birnam Wood
  Shall we well meet them; that way are they coming.

CAITHNESS.   Who knows if Donalbain be with his brother?

LENNOX.   For certain, sir, he is not. I have a file°
  Of all the gentry. There is Siward's son   10
  And many unrough° youths that even now
  Protest° their first° of manhood.

---

64 **Infected** (with guilt)
66 **divine** priest
68 **annoyance** self-injury
69 **still** constantly
70 **mated** stunned, overcome (with perhaps a glance at the chess sense)
V ii 1 **pow'r** army
3 **dear** heartfelt
3 **causes** reasons for action, i.e. griefs
4 **the bleeding** i.e. battle (but with a pun on bleeding in the older medical sense of

treating a malady by relieving the patient of some of his blood)
4 **grim alarm** (of war)
5 **mortified** i.e. even the dead
9 **file** list
11 **unrough** beardless
12 **Protest** proclaim
12 **first** i.e. first test by battle

MENTEITH.   What does the tyrant?

CAITHNESS.   Great Dunsinane he strongly fortifies.
Some say he's mad; others, that lesser hate him,   15
Do call it valiant fury; but for certain
He cannot buckle his distempered° cause
Within the belt of rule.°

ANGUS.   Now does he feel
His secret murders sticking on his hands.   20
Now minutely° revolts° upbraid his faith-breach.
Those he commands move only in command,
Nothing° in love. Now does he feel his title
Hang loose about him, like a giant's robe
Upon a dwarfish thief.   25

MENTEITH.   Who then shall blame
His pestered° senses to recoil and start,
When all that is within him does condemn
Itself for being there?

CAITHNESS.   Well, march we on   30
To give obedience where 'tis truly owed.
Meet we° the med'cine° of the sickly weal;°
And with him pour we in our country's purge°
Each drop of us.

LENNOX.   Or so much as it needs   35
To dew° the sovereign flower° and drown the weeds.
Make we our march towards Birnam.   *Exeunt, marching.*

---

17 **distempered** diseased, in this case
swollen (as with dropsy)
17-18 **buckle . . . rule** (1) restore his diseased, anarchic kingdom to law and order
(?) (2) restore his own sick and unruly self
to sanity (see "mad," 15) (?)
21 **minutely** at every minute
21 **revolts** rebellions
23 **Nothing** not at all
27 **pestered** tormented
32 **Meet we** let us meet
32 **med'cine** i.e. Malcolm

32 **weal** wealth, i.e. commonwealth
33 **purge** purification (the image is of a
purgative medicine compounded of the
blood shed by the opponents of tyranny in
the forthcoming battle)
36 **dew** water
36 **the . . . flower** i.e. the true monarchy
(with the further implication that true monarchy will be curative—"sovereign flower"
in the sense of sovereign herb, i.e. effica-
cious remedy)

Enter Macbeth, Doctor, and Attendants.   V ii

MACBETH.   Bring me no more reports. Let them fly all!°
    Till Birnam Wood remove to Dunsinane,
    I cannot taint° with fear. What's the boy Malcolm?
    Was he not born of woman? The spirits that know
    All mortal consequences° have pronounced me thus: 5
    "Fear not, Macbeth. No man that's born of woman
    Shall e'er have power upon thee." Then fly, false thanes,
    And mingle with the English epicures.°
    The mind I sway° by and the heart I bear
    Shall never sag with doubt nor shake with fear.   10

Enter Servant.

    The devil damn thee black, thou cream-faced° loon!
    Where got'st thou that goose look?

SERVANT.   There is ten thousand—

MACBETH.   Geese, villain?

SERVANT.   Soldiers, sir.   15

MACBETH.   Go prick thy face and over-red° thy fear,
    Thou lily-livered boy. What soldiers, patch?°
    Death of thy soul!° those linen° cheeks of thine
    Are counsellors to fear. What soldiers, whey-face?°

SERVANT.   The English force, so please you.   20

MACBETH.   Take thy face hence. [*Exit Servant.*] Seyton!—I am
    sick at heart,
    When I behold—Seyton, I say!—This push°
    Will cheer me ever, or disseat me now.
    I have lived long enough. My way of life

V iii **1 Bring . . . all** (Macbeth has been hearing of successive defections of his supporters)
3 taint become contaminated (more specifically, this may signify "wither" (OED, 3b) or "rot" (OED, 4b), or here, though there appears to be no OED warrant for the intransitive in this sense, "change color," "go pale"; much is later made in this scene of the *color* of fear, 11-19)
5 mortal consequences ordained sequences of events that govern in mortal life (but for the audience the further sense of **mortal as** deathbringing may also be implicit, since the ordained succession of events that Macbeth counts on to protect him will ruin him)
8 epicures i.e. as contrasted with the frugal Scots
9 sway rule myself
11 cream-faced i.e. white from fear
16 over-red cover with red blood
17 patch fool
18 Death . . . soul death take thy soul
18 linen i.e. white
19 whey-face (whey is the watery white milk left after the curds have been separated out in the making of cheese)
22 push supreme effort

Is fall'n into the sear,° the yellow leaf,   25
And that which should accompany old age,
As honor, love, obedience, troops of friends,
I must not look° to have; but, in their stead,
Curses not loud but deep, mouth-honor, breath,
Which the poor heart would fain deny, and dare not.   30
Seyton!

Enter Seyton.

SEYTON.   What's your gracious pleasure?

MACBETH.   What news more?

SEYTON.   All is confirmed, my lord, which was reported.

MACBETH.   I'll fight till from my bones my flesh be hacked.   35
Give me my armor.

SEYTON.   'Tis not needed yet.

MACBETH.   I'll put it on.
Send out moe° horses, skirr° the country round,
Hang those that talk of fear. Give me mine armor.   40
How does your patient, doctor?

DOCTOR.   Not so sick, my lord,
As she is troubled° with thick-coming fancies
That keep her from her rest.

MACBETH.   Cure her of that!   45
Canst thou not minister to a mind diseased,
Pluck from the memory a rooted sorrow,
Raze out° the written troubles of the brain,
And with some sweet oblivious° antidote
Cleanse the stuffed° bosom of that perilous stuff   50
Which weighs upon the heart?

DOCTOR.   Therein the patient
Must minister to himself.

MACBETH.   Throw physic° to the dogs, I'll none of it!
Come, put mine armor on. Give me my staff.   55
Seyton, send out.°—Doctor, the thanes fly from me.—

---

25 **the sear** the withered phase, i.e. its
autumn
28 **look** expect
39 **moe** more
39 **skirr** scour
42-43 **Not . . . troubled** not so much
really sick as troubled

48 **Raze out** erase
49 **oblivious** bringing forgetfulness
50 **stuffed** clogged
54 **physic** the art of medicine
56 **send out** see 39

Come, sir, dispatch.°—If thou couldst, doctor, cast
The water° of my land, find her disease,
And purge it to a sound and pristine° health,
I would applaud thee to the very echo,°   60
That should applaud again.—Pull't° off, I say.—
What rhubarb, cyme,° or what purgative drug
Would scour these English hence? Hear'st thou of them?

DOCTOR.   Ay, my good lord. Your royal preparation
Makes us hear something.   65

MACBETH.   Bring it° after me!
I will not be afraid of death and bane°
Till Birnam Forest come to Dunsinane.

Exeunt [all but the Doctor.]

DOCTOR.   Were I from Dunsinane away and clear,
Profit again should hardly draw me here.   *[Exit.]* 70

◦◦◦◦◦◦◦

Drum and Colors. Enter Malcolm, Siward, Macduff,   V i
Siward's Son, Menteith, Caithness, Angus,
[Lennox, Ross,] and Soldiers, marching.

MALCOLM.   Cousins, I hope the days are near at hand
That chambers° will be safe.

MENTEITH.   We doubt it nothing.°

SIWARD.   What wood is this before us?

MENTEITH.   The Wood of Birnam.   5

MALCOLM.   Let every soldier hew him down a bough
And bear't before him. Thereby shall we shadow°

---

57 **dispatch** make haste (spoken to Seyton, who is arming him)
57-58 **cast The water** analyze the urine
59 **pristine** old-time
60 **to . . . echo** i.e. till the applause
echoed
61 **'t** it, i.e. a piece of armor that he has
got on wrong
62 **cyme** the tender tip of the cabbage
plant, which was held to have purgative

effects (some editors take the word to be a
mispelling of "cynne," an old spelling of
"senna"—also a purgative)
66 **it** i.e. his armor
67 **bane** destruction (possibly with the
specific meaning of murder—see OED, bane,
sb. 1 and 3)
V iv 2 chambers bedrooms
3 **nothing** not at all
7 **shadow** conceal

The numbers of our host and make discovery°
    Err in report of us.

SOLDIERS.   It shall be done.   10

SIWARD.   We learn no other but the confident tyrant
    Keeps still in Dunsinane and will endure°
    Our setting down before't.°

MALCOLM.   'Tis his main hope,
    For where there is advantage to be given°   15
    Both more and less° have given him the revolt,
    And none serve with him but constrainèd things
    Whose hearts are absent too.

MACDUFF.   Let our just censures°
    Attend° the true event,° and put we on   20
    Industrious soldiership.

SIWARD.   The time approaches
    That will with due decision make us know
    What we shall say we have and what we owe.°
    Thoughts speculative their unsure hopes relate,   25
    But certain issue strokes must arbitrate—
    Towards which advance the war.°   *Exeunt, marching.*

⌁⌁⌁

Enter Macbeth, Seyton, and Soldiers, with Drum and Colors.   V v

MACBETH.   Hang out our banners on the outward walls.
    The cry is still, "They come!" Our castle's strength
    Will laugh a siege to scorn. Here let them lie
    Till famine and the ague° eat them up.
    Were they not forced° with those that should be ours,   5

---

8 **discovery** reconnaissance
12 **endure** allow
13 **setting . . . before't** laying siege to it
15 **there . . . given** opportunity is offered
16 **more and less** nobles and commoners
19 **censures** i.e. judgments (of the weakness of Macbeth's side)
20 **Attend** await
20 **event** outcome

24 **owe** own, i.e. really have (as compared to verbal claims)
25-27 **Thoughts . . . war** speculation has only unsure hopes to offer us; the actual outcome will be decided in the battle, towards which let us now advance our troops
V v 4 **ague** fever
5 **forced** reinforced

We might have met them dareful,° beard to beard,
And beat them backward home. (*A cry within of women.*)
    What is that noise?

SEYTON.   It is the cry of women, my good lord.   [*Exit.*]

MACBETH.   I have almost forgot the taste of fears.
    The time has been my senses would have cooled   10
    To hear a night-shriek, and my fell° of hair
    Would at a dismal treatise° rouse and stir
    As° life were in't. I have supped full with horrors.°
    Direness,° familiar to my slaughterous thoughts,
    Cannot once start° me. [*Enter Seyton.*] Wherefore was that   15
    cry?

SEYTON.   The Queen, my lord, is dead.

MACBETH.   She should have died hereafter:
    There would have been a time for such a word.°
    To-morrow, and to-morrow, and to-morrow
    Creeps in this petty pace from day to day   20
    To the last syllable of recorded time,
    And all our yesterdays have lighted fools
    The way to dusty death. Out, out, brief candle!
    Life's but a walking shadow, a poor player
    That struts and frets his hour upon the stage   25
    And then is heard no more. It is a tale
    Told by an idiot, full of sound and fury,
    Signifying nothing.

                        Enter a Messenger.

    Thou com'st to use thy tongue: thy story quickly!

MESSENGER.   Gracious my lord,   30
    I should report that which I say I saw,
    But know not how to do't.

---

6 dareful boldly
11 fell pelt, i.e. skin with the hair on (here, probably, scalp)
12 treatise story
13 As as if
13 with horrors on horrors (but perhaps "with horrors" is also meant to call up images of the terrifying guest at Macbeth's table)
14 Direness horror
15 start startle
17-18 She . . . word this may be taken to mean either (1) that her death should have

come at another time; there would have been a more suitable moment for such news; or (2) that she would have died eventually anyway; a day was certainly bound to come bringing such a message; the latter sense seems to suit better the spirit of Macbeth's soliloquy, where the morrows creep on emptily and as they pass into yesterdays bring the fools that all men are to their deaths

MACBETH.   Well, say, sir.

MESSENGER.   As I did stand my watch upon the hill,
  I looked toward Birnam, and anon methought   35
  The wood began to move.

MACBETH.   Liar and slave!

MESSENGER.   Let me endure your wrath if't be not so.
  Within this three mile may you see it coming.
  I say, a moving grove.   40

MACBETH.   If thou speak'st false,
  Upon the next tree shalt thou hang alive
  Till famine cling° thee. If thy speech be sooth,°
  I care not if thou dost for me as much.
  I pull in resolution,° and begin   45
  To doubt° th' equivocation of the fiend,
  That lies like truth. "Fear not, till Birnam Wood
  Do come to Dunsinane!" and now a wood
  Comes toward Dunsinane. Arm, arm, and out!
  If this which he avouches° does appear,   50
  There is nor flying hence nor tarrying here.
  I 'gin to be aweary of the sun,
  And wish th' estate o' th' world° were now undone.
  Ring the alarum bell! Blow wind, come wrack,°
  At least we'll die with harness° on our back.   *Exeunt.* 55

———

Drum and Colors. Enter Malcolm, Siward,   V vi
Macduff, and their Army, with boughs.

MALCOLM.   Now near enough.
  Your leavy° screens throw down.
  And show° like those you are. You, worthy uncle,°

---

43 **cling** shrivel
43 **sooth** truth
45 **pull in resolution** rein in my confidence
46 **doubt** suspect
50 **avouches** asserts
53 **estate . . . world** the whole frame of
things

54 **wrack** ruin
55 **harness** armor
V vi 2 **leavy** leafy
3 **show** appear
3 **uncle** Siward

Shall with my cousin, your right noble son,°
Lead our first battle.° Worthy Macduff and we   5
Shall take upon's° what else remains to do,
According to our order.°

SIWARD.   Fare you well.
Do we° but find the tyrant's power° to-night,
Let us be beaten if we cannot fight.   10

MACDUFF.   Make all our trumpets speak, give them all breath,
Those clamorous harbingers of blood and death.

Exeunt. Alarums continued.

❦

Enter Macbeth.   V *vi*

MACBETH.   They have tied me to a stake. I cannot fly,
But bear-like I must fight the course.° What's he
That was not born of woman? Such a one
Am I to fear, or none.

Enter Young Siward.

YOUNG SIWARD.   What is thy name?   5

MACBETH.   Thou'lt be afraid to hear it.

YOUNG SIWARD.   No, though thou call'st thyself a hotter name
Than any is in hell.

MACBETH.   My name's Macbeth.

YOUNG SIWARD.   The devil himself could not pronounce a title   10
More hateful to mine ear.

MACBETH.   No, nor more fearful.

YOUNG SIWARD.   Thou liest, abhorrèd tyrant! With my sword
I'll prove the lie thou speak'st.

Fight, and Young Siward slain.

---

4 **son** young Siward
5 **battle** battalion
6 **upon's** upon us
7 **order** plan
9 **Do we** if we do

9 **power** forces
V vii 1-2 **They . . . course** i.e. like a bear
tied to a stake to be baited by dogs, I
must fight this bout to the end

MACBETH.   Thou wast born of woman.   15
    But swords I smile at, weapons laugh to scorn,
    Brandished by man that's of a woman born.   *Exit.*

            Alarums. Enter Macduff.

MACDUFF.   That way the noise is. Tyrant, show thy face!
    If thou beest slain and with no stroke of mine,
    My wife and children's ghosts will haunt me still.   20
    I cannot strike at wretched kerns,° whose arms
    Are hired to bear their staves.° Either thou,° Macbeth,
    Or else my sword with an unbattered edge
    I sheathe again undeeded.° There thou shouldst be:
    By this great clatter one of greatest note   25
    Seems bruited.° Let me find him, Fortune,
    And more I beg not!   *Exit. Alarums.*

            Enter Malcolm and Siward.

SIWARD.   This way, my lord. The castle's gently rend'red:°
    The tyrant's people on both sides do fight,
    The noble thanes do bravely in the war,   30
    The day almost itself professes° yours
    And little is to do.

MALCOLM.   We have met with foes
    That strike beside us.°

SIWARD.   Enter, sir, the castle.   *Exeunt. Alarum.* 35

                          ◦◦◦

           Enter Macbeth.   V viii

MACBETH.   Why should I play the Roman fool° and die
    On mine own sword? Whiles I see lives,° the gashes
    Do better upon them.

---

21 **wretched kerns** mere peasants—see note
I ii 15
22 **staves** spears
22 **Either thou** either I fight you
24 **undeeded** without its having performed
any deeds
26 **bruited** noised, indicated
28 **gently rend'red** surrendered with little
opposition

31 **professes** declares
34 **strike beside us** (1) take our side (?)
(2) strike to miss us (?)
V viii 1 Roman fool e.g. any of the Roman statesmen who took their own lives
when defeated: Cato, Brutus, Antony, etc.
2 **lives** living men

Enter Macduff.

MACDUFF.   Turn, hellhound, turn!

MACBETH.   Of all men else I have avoided thee.   5
But get thee back! My soul is too much charged°
With blood of thine already.

MACDUFF.   I have no words;
My voice is in my sword, thou bloodier villain
Than terms can give thee out!°   *Fight. Alarum.* 10

MACBETH.   Thou losest labor.
As easy mayst thou the intrenchant° air
With thy keen sword impress° as make me bleed.
Let fall thy blade on vulnerable crests.
I bear a charmèd life, which must not yield   15
To one of woman born.

MACDUFF.   Despair thy charm,
And let the angel° whom thou still° hast served
Tell thee, Macduff was from his mother's womb
Untimely ripped.   20

MACBETH.   Accursèd be that tongue that tells me so,
For it hath cowed my better part° of man!
And be these juggling fiends no more believed,
That palter° with us in a double sense,
That keep the word of promise to our ear   25
And break it to our hope. I'll not fight with thee.

MACDUFF.   Then yield thee, coward,
And live to be the show and gaze° o' th' time.
We'll have thee, as our rarer monsters are,
Painted upon a pole,° and underwrit   30
"Here may you see the tyrant."

MACBETH.   I will not yield,
To kiss the ground before young Malcolm's feet
And to be baited° with the rabble's curse.
Though Birnam Wood be come to Dunsinane,   35

---

6 **charged** burdened
10 **Than . . . out** than words can express
12 **intrenchant** uncuttable
13 **impress** make an impression on
18 **angel** fallen angel, i.e. demon
18 **still** always
22 **better part** i.e. mind

24 **palter** equivocate
28 **gaze** spectacle
30 **upon a pole** i.e. on a board or banner set up. on a pole to advertise a show of freaks (as today at a fair or circus)
34 **baited** see note V vii 1-2

And thou opposed, being of no woman born,
Yet I will try the last.° Before my body
I throw my warlike shield. Lay on, Macduff,
And damned be him that first cries "Hold, enough!"

> *Exeunt fighting. Alarums.*

> [*Re-*]*enter fighting, and Macbeth slain.* [*Exit Macduff.*]
> *Retreat and flourish. Enter, with Drum and Colors,*
> *Malcolm, Siward, Ross, Thanes, and Soldiers.*

MALCOLM.   I would the friends we miss were safe arrived.   40

SIWARD.   Some must go off;° and yet, by these I see,°
So great a day as this is cheaply bought.

MALCOLM.   Macduff is missing, and your noble son.

ROSS.   Your son, my lord, has paid a soldier's debt.
He only lived but till he was a man,   45
The which no sooner had his prowess confirmed
In the unshrinking station° where he fought
But like a man he died.

SIWARD.   Then he is dead?

ROSS.   Ay, and brought off the field. Your cause of sorrow   50
Must not be measured by his worth, for then
It hath no end.

SIWARD.   Had he his hurts before?

ROSS.   Ay, on the front.

SIWARD.   Why then, God's soldier be he.   55
Had I as many sons as I have hairs,°
I would not wish them to a fairer death:
And so his knell is knolled.

MALCOLM.   He's worth more sorrow,
And that I'll spend for him.   60

SIWARD.   He's worth no more.
They say he parted° well and paid his score,°
And so, God be with him. Here comes newer comfort.

> *Enter Macduff, with Macbeth's head.*

---

37 **try the last** (1) give all I have left (?)
(2) fight to the last or even if I am the
last (?)   (3) test this invulnerability you receive from "being of no woman born" (?)
41 **go off** i.e. die
41 **these I see** these survivors

47 **unshrinking station** i.e. the frontline
post he never shrank from
56 **hairs** (with a pun on "heirs")
62 **parted** departed, died
62 **paid his score** paid up his account

MACDUFF.   Hail, King, for so thou art.
  Behold where stands   65
  Th' usurper's cursèd head. The time is free.
  I see thee compassed° with thy kingdom's pearl,°
  That speak my salutation in their minds,
  Whose voices I desire aloud with mine—
  Hail, King of Scotland!   70

ALL.   Hail, King of Scotland!   *Flourish.*

MALCOLM.   We shall not spend a large expense of time
  Before we reckon with° your several° loves
  And make us even with you. My Thanes and kinsmen,
  Henceforth be Earls, the first that ever Scotland 75
  In such an honor named. What's more to do
  Which would be planted newly with the time°—
  As calling home our exiled friends abroad
  That fled the snares of watchful tyranny,
  Producing forth the cruel ministers°   80
  Of this dead butcher and his fiend-like queen,
  Who (as 'tis thought) by self and violent hands
  Took off her life—this, and what needful else
  That calls upon us,° by the grace of Grace°
  We will perform in measure, time, and place.° 85
  So thanks to all at once and to each one,
  Whom we invite to see us crowned at Scone.

        Flourish. Exeunt omnes.

---

67 **compassed** encompassed
67 **pearl** i.e. jewels (his loyal thanes)
73 **reckon with** reward
73 **several** individual
76-77 **What's . . . time** other things which need to be done at the outset of this new era

80 **ministers** agents
84 **calls upon us** demands our attention
84 **Grace** i.e. God
85 **in . . . place** fittingly at the fitting time and place

IN THE THEATER OF THE MIND

i

The comments that follow are meant to suggest ways of internally *visualizing* and *feeling* the play, which are essential if the reading of it is not to be merely an intellectual exercise. Few of us get a chance to see professional productions of Shakespeare, and that's a pity; the lines well spoken, the parts well acted have a profound impact that is hard to duplicate in the study. Nevertheless, the life of a Shakespearean play *is* in the lines, and an imaginative reader can realize that life in the theater of his own mind. Shakespeare's Globe demanded of the audience a ready ear and an inward eye—a willingness to transcend what they saw before them in order to transform it imaginatively into a world that neither eye nor ear actually quite caught. A reader can do the same, and, once he has learned how, is better off in doing it for himself by the activity of his own imagination than he is in passively allowing a stage or film director to do it for him. Even the greatest of professional productions remains subject, in the end, to the image of the play's potentialities that exists in a seasoned playgoer's, or a seasoned reader's, mind.

Since we are not directly concerned here with how the play should be produced in the theater, but rather with how parts of it may be realized in the imagination, we refer to actual staging only to point out what the language indicates is going on inside and outside the characters. On the same grounds, we make no attempt to "cover" the total action in any chronological way. Our observations on particular scenes are intended to suggest ways of looking at others as well.

ii

To see *Macbeth* in the theater of the mind, it is necessary to recognize the overarching moral order of the Macbeths' world within which their assault on that order takes its terrible toll. It's a world undergirded by moral imperatives, and we aren't allowed to forget that fact, even with the sense of Evil and nihilism that permeates the play. It may be tempting to make psychological case studies out of Macbeth and Lady Macbeth, but this is not a problem play with everyday people working out everyday problems. The Macbeths are all too human, but in a larger-than-life sense. There is no point in asking, "Why did they do it?" That is a question easily answered ("They wanted the throne"), but at the same time impossible to answer (What is it in us that makes us want thrones and from what sources does that want spring?). The focus of the play is precisely on the mystery of their doing it at all and on the mystery of what happens to them while and after doing it. The play acts out the dreadful reality of human beings caught up in warring against their own natures and against Nature itself in a universe conceived of as a battleground.

So strong is the sense of obscure powers in conflict everywhere in the play that some directors have sought to give them a concrete definition in stage symbols—a wall-niche with a Madonna image, let's say, on one side of the stage, a throne on the other, each standing for a different conception of power, each always dimly visible to the audience, but lit up warmly at appropriate moments, the Madonna relating to all those elements in the play that have to do with healing, renewing, green branches, children, hope, and the throne to all those images that cause destruction and despair. With modern lighting, such objects can appear at one moment as what they are, at another moment as rocks or parts of walls. Particularization of the conflict in terms as specific as these is nowhere required by the play, but is sometimes useful in helping us to see how polarized between mysterious forces that are basically good and mysterious forces that are basically evil most of its action is and how appropriately therefore it is stretched like a fine taut web between opening and concluding battles.

The very first scene of only thirteen lines establishes a mystery that we gather is also sinister. Thunder—lightning—

three strange apparitions that appear and disappear like personi-
fied ominous hints of something yet to be more fully known,
waiting for Macbeth. The apparitions seem to know when the
battle will be over, even while it's going on. They seem to know
that it will be lost *and* won, not lost *or* won, as if they were
introducing us to a world where winning is always loss and
loss is winning. ("For what is a man profited, if he shall gain
the whole world and lose his own soul?" Matthew 16:26). Yet
more ominous is the fact that it seems to be a world in which
ordinary values are reversed: "Fair is foul, and foul is fair." For
what imaginable beings, human or otherwise, could this possibly
be true, we wonder? And why, suddenly, are we—or they—in a
suffocating atmosphere of "fog and filthy air"? No matter what
may be one's ability to conjure up these sinister riddling presences, or a director's ability to make us see and sense them,
the power of the scene lies in its tantalizing ambiguities. And
when it fades, it leaves another riddle in its stead: a "bloody
man" in place of the three swirling females. What does *he* have
to do with *them*? Is he their opposite or their agent? Or a
symbol of all that is to come?

The "bleeding captain" will tell his story, heedless of his
wounds, because the great victory of Macbeth overrides all
other considerations. The whole scene is a paean to Macbeth's
virtues—and by extension to the virtues of loyalty and order.
Macbeth has been often enough interpreted as a man *guilty
before* the play begins. It seems more in keeping with the evidence to say instead that he is *susceptible as* the play begins:
he is in the position of any ambitious man who wonders (and
hopes?) what his success may bring. The openness here—of
blunt language, of reports of direct physical confrontation, of
honest praising of heroic exploits, of respect for duty and service—must be seen in luminous contrast to the obscurity of the
preceding scene and the turmoil and uncertainty of the following one. Macbeth, up to this point, *is* all that he's reported to be,
and the others in the scene honor him for it, yet lose no honor
of their own in doing so. The scene must be visualized and
played as such to underscore the enormity of what is soon to
come, what is already (as scene i possibly implies) in transit;
and the rest of Act I will complete the counterpoint: scenes
iii, v, and vii as the faces of Evil, surrounding ii, iv, and vi, the
faces of Good. Changes of time or place make little difference.

The scene changes flow one into the other in a continuum—holy order contending with unholy disorder, and at the close of the act defeated, though here as elsewhere in a loss that will eventually prove a winning.

iii

Act II is the act of darkness, a descent into spiritual Hell, intensified, not relieved, by the ghoulish humor of the drunken porter. After Banquo and Fleance go to bed, Macbeth is left alone, waiting the agreed-on signal. On the instant, he sees before him the "fatal vision" of a dagger, the "handle toward [his] hand," a further convulsion of his tortured conscience, so vividly revealed in the verbal projections of Act I. The recoil of his moral being against the murder expresses itself in an active visualization of every circumstance that the act entails: the murderous weapon, the movement of his own body in the fatal direction of Duncan's room ("Thou marshall'st me the way that I was going" [50], he says), and now upon the blade and handle the actual drops of blood. In his *mind* the deed is already done. Then with one agonized gesture, he pushes the vision away: "There's no such thing./It is the bloody business which informs/Thus to mine eyes" (55-57). In a kind of somnambulism, as if he were moving in a nightmare and verbally drawing the fearful images of nightmare around him—"wicked dream," "witchcraft," "withered Murder," "the wolf," "ravishing" Tarquin, the "ghost"—he walks unsteadily to his exit, setting each foot down as if it were not quite his own; for the implication that his members are at war with each other, the consequence of his "multiplying villainies" against Duncan, is the most recurrent image of the play. As he nears the exit, he hears the signal bell ring, telling him that his "drink" is ready. He gives a shudder, for he knows what that drink is going to be made of, and then is gone. If there is a visible throne on the stage, Macbeth should be looking at it when he dismisses the dagger as a mirage; for here is something that is not a mirage. He may also be imagined as casting one long intense look back at it as he exits to Duncan's room.

The next scene, II ii, is a terrible ordeal for participants and audience alike. Sometimes it has been conceived to take place almost wholly in mutterings and whispers; sometimes with a protagonist and wife who, after his initial entrance, never look each other directly in the face. Their responses to what he has done couldn't be more different: his imagination runs wild, hers is matter of fact. When he enters, muttering in a strangled tone, "I have done the deed./ Didst thou not hear a noise?" she replies only that she has heard an owl shriek and crickets sing. When he exclaims, terrified, and with the moral question uppermost, "I could not say 'Amen!'/When they did say 'God bless us!' " she tells him this is to consider too deeply. When he speaks of the voice that cried, "Sleep no more./Macbeth does murder sleep," she calls his behavior "brainsickly." As she starts to put her hand on him to reassure him, she notices the blood and the daggers. This time she must take a still tighter grip on herself: "go carry them," she says, "and smear/ The sleepy grooms with blood." Macbeth can't face it. "Give me the daggers," she says. "The sleeping and the dead/Are but as pictures. 'Tis the eye of childhood/That fears a painted devil."

While she is gone, the knock that comes paralyzes him. He is too unstrung to hide, and only the porter's drunkenness saves him from discovery. He stands there with his hands jerking as if they were not under his own control: "What hands are here?" he mutters, "Ha! they pluck out mine eyes." Here again is an indication of the revolt within his "single state of man" that has been developing from the beginning. Then he thinks of getting rid of the blood, but makes no move, for he knows inwardly that blood in *his* sense is never to be gotten rid of: "No, this my hand will rather/The multitudinous seas incarnadine,/Making the green one red." But blood in Lady Macbeth's sense is easy to get rid of: "A little water clears us of this deed." Unlike him, who is transfixed by the knock on the door as if it were a supernatural summons, she locates it matter of factly "at the south entry." She now talks to him reassuringly, rapidly, telling him what to do, while he remains standing as if in a trance. In acting the play, the rest of this scene becomes enormously suspenseful if, with growing alarm, she struggles to arouse him, tugs at his arm to bring him to his senses, and finally pulls him offstage, as if he were a tell-tale corpse that had to be removed from the scene of the crime—he still murmuring in a lifeless and faraway voice as though from another world: "Wake Duncan with thy knocking!/I would thou couldst." If there is any visible stage symbol of the healing and creative force in the play, it will be seen to shine faintly during Macbeth's sleep speeches and to go abruptly out when Lady Macbeth lumps the sleeping with the dead. But as the knocking grows in clamor in the long suspenseful interval before the porter enters, the symbol, whatever it is, should be clearly lit.

Though the knocking cannot wake Duncan, it will remind us who are "watchers" that this "most bloody piece of work" is about to come to light. In a superb dramatic touch, Shakespeare creates a besotted doorman—again, like the bleeding captain, a mysterious figure whom we see but once—to play a silly game of "knock-knock" as an unconscious but deadly commentary on what has just occurred. His three imaginary candidates for admission to hell have all but outsmarted ("o'erleaped" is Macbeth's word) themselves, as have the Macbeths with their "vaulting ambition." The juxtaposition of their sleazy activities with the enormity of murdering one's liege lord and guest puts the latter event in the most gruesome light possible, and also allows the everyday world to flow back on to the stage so that it can again be shattered by horror, this time the horror of the discovery.

When Macbeth enters to greet Macduff and Lennox, it appears to them that their knocking has awakened him,. and we see him now in tight control of himself: crisp, polite, but, in terms of the cross-bow image (I vii 89 and II ii 54) "bent" to the snapping point. Macduff rushes back from Duncan's chamber shouting his dismay, and Macbeth, rather than be scrutinized in the spotlight of that moment, hurries to the chamber with Lennox. But the tension rises, and when he returns, there is no longer any ducking it. Now, too, the stage is suddenly exploding with people from all directions, as if in a miniature Last Judgment—in the center, surrounded by rank on rank of frightened and then questioning faces, the two Macbeths.

Macbeth's words at this point are both dissembling and profoundly prophetic of his deepest self: "Had I but died an hour before this chance,/I had lived a blessèd time; for from this instant/There's nothing serious in mortality." He feels all eyes on him, and he protests too much. He confesses that he killed the grooms, and when Macduff asks, quite naturally, "Wherefore did you so?" he starts off, "Who can be wise, amazed, temp'rate and furious,/Loyal and neutral, in a moment?" It is an overwrought response, and he rushes on to further justification in the same vein. Whether Lady Macbeth's faint is genuine or cleverly faked to draw attention away from him is not certain, but Macbeth wisely grasps the chance to attend her and shut himself off. Malcolm and Donalbain seize the moment also to tell each other that they are next in blood in more ways than one ("The near in blood, The nearer bloody"), and the scene ends in disorder and mistrust: "Fears and scruples [doubts] shake us," says Banquo in a masterpiece of understatement. Sometimes, just as the two boys run off-stage, Macbeth is shown at the top of the castle staircase, alert suddenly to a reaction on their part that he has not foreseen.

iv

Acts III and IV orchestrate the corrosive power of evil upon those who knowingly choose it and upon the world they victimize. The focus is on Macbeth, King of Scotland now through the reality of living terror, but also King of Darkness through the onset of spiritual death. At the opening of Act III, we can see already that the man who dissimulated so badly in the scene after Duncan's murder has come a long way. He is even so suave now that he dares throw in an ironic reminder to Banquo: "Fail not our feast." Banquo's reply, "My lord, I will not," is one to make Macbeth smile inwardly; but the smile is premature: Banquo *does* come to the feast.

After Banquo departs for his afternoon ride, we get a good look at the new King's face for the first time. It is haggard and drawn, because he has not slept. It makes an ironic contrast with the great throne in the background, with the sumptuousness of the royal surroundings and the splendid robes, pointing up the emptiness of his achievement and the weariness of his words after the rest have gone out: "To be thus is nothing, but to be safely thus." The logic of this speech is interesting. It starts out with what appears to be a fear that Banquo, suspecting the truth, will overthrow him; but it becomes rapidly clear that this is not the real difficulty, or if so, only a part of it. The real difficulty is Banquo's character and his destiny, and it is these facts that move Macbeth to murder. What Macbeth sees in Banquo is a reminder of the futility of his crime. He wants to kill that sense of futility too, so that he can sleep.

Further signs of his deterioration appear in his interview with the murderers in III i and with his wife in III ii. With the murderers, he has spun a web of falsification such that these poor country gentry, down on their luck, attribute their misfortunes to Banquo, and he spurs them on with the same redefinition of man that he was once, himself, reluctant to accept. "Ay, in the catalogue ye go for men," he says to them, but the test of manhood is whether you are willing to assassinate an enemy; now if you have that kind of manhood, "say't;/ And I will put that business in your bosoms/Whose execution takes your enemy off"—and earns my love. We can hardly help remembering Lady Macbeth's "When you durst do it, then you were a man" (I vii 54).

His relations with his wife have greatly changed. Her face in III ii is like Macbeth's, drawn and sleepless. She too realizes that the achievement they have made is empty: "Naught's had, all's spent." But what is noteworthy in her is that the once steely will is slack. She has not even been party to the plan for *this* murder; she is merely told of it by hints. Where she dominated him, in the scene of Duncan's death, he now dominates her. Where she had to take his hand and almost pull him from the stage at that time, he now takes hers and draws her after: "Thou marvell'st at my words, but hold thee still"—that is, no effort is required on your part; "Things bad begun make strong themselves by ill."

The most striking of all these stages of Macbeth's deterioration, in theatrical terms, is the scene with Banquo's ghost. The ghost is, of course, a real person as far as the audience is concerned: if he were not they would have no idea what Macbeth is talking about when he turns to sit down and finds the table full. But the ghost is seen by no other character except Macbeth, and one may conclude from his wife's words that we are supposed to think of it as in some sense a final outraged protest by his conscience, like the previous images: "This is the very painting of your fear," she says—as she had also said of his earlier visionary experience; "This is the air-drawn dagger which you said/Led you to Duncan." For Macbeth on the other hand it is all too real, and even after he has willed it away with a supreme effort twice, he still turns and says, in the hearing of the assembled guests: How can you "behold such sights/And keep the natural ruby of your cheeks/When mine is blanched with fear"? Even after the guests are gone, he stands there staring and muttering: "It will have blood, they say:/Blood will have blood." And blood will. For when he comes to his senses, with his conscience now put behind him for the last time, his mind is already on Macduff.

v

Act V is the act of retribution, the dismembering of Evil, the triumph of light over darkness, the restitution of order in the temporal and spiritual worlds. The preceding acts have been a kind of nightmare in terms of blood and darkness. Here at the beginning of Act V is that nightmare in an altogether literal sense, a vision of hell internalized. The doctor of the scene is calculated to remind us of the doctor in the Edward the Confessor episode of the scene before. There, healing was possible because of Edward's divine grace; here, healing is impossible because there is no divine grace: "More needs she the divine than the physician" the Doctor says. Lady Macbeth has often, we hear, since Macbeth went out into the field, got up and written letters in her sleep—in an effort, one takes it, to get rid of guilt by a confession. She never has been without a light beside her because the darkness she used to invoke terrifies her now. When she has set her candle down, she leans over a desk, washing. "A little water clears us of the deed," she had been used to say. Now she says, with a low moan, as a child might, holding her hands beside the candle and gazing at them intently: "Yet here's a spot." Wearily she resumes washing, then lifts her head, for she hears again the bell she struck for Duncan's murder: "One—two—why then 'tis time to do't." Lifting an imaginary dagger, she starts forward, but glancing downward at the bed, recoils—as if it *were* her father in his sleep, or as if it were the brink of hell.

She used to think, as did her husband, that she could "jump the life to come"; now she says with a gasp, "Hell is murky," and we realize with a start what atmosphere that was in the play's first scene when the witches hovered through the "fog and filthy air." Then we see the terror fade from her face, to be followed by contempt: "Fie, my lord, fie! a soldier and afeard?" And this is followed by what we may suppose to be a look of arrogance: "What need we fear who knows it, when

none can call our pow'r to accompt?" But then comes the con-
vulsive shuddering: "Yet who would have thought the old man
to have had so much blood in him?" As the shudder dies away,
it is replaced, we may again imagine, by an expression of profound sadness. Like a woman rocking a child asleep and singing
a nursery tune, she murmurs: "The Thane of Fife had a wife.
Where is she now?" and possibly she reaches out her hand as
if she would stroke the head of an imaginary infant. At any
rate, she sees her hand again, and once more resumes her
washing: "What, will these hands ne'er be clean?" After a
while, she looks up with a start as if she had heard someone:
"No more o' that, my lord, no more o' that! You mar all with
this starting"—she is remembering the past and Banquo's ghost.
But the washing goes on. When she stretches out her hands
finally to the candle, a faint smile of relief starts to creep across
her face, but then as she bends down more closely, she recoils
again: "Here's the smell of the blood still." Then she turns
abruptly, motioning to somebody but without looking at him:
"Wash your hands, put on your nightgown, look not so pale!"
She is remembering the knocking at the gate. Then her tone
firms as she remembers a different scene: "I tell you yet again,
Banquo's buried. He cannot come out on's grave." Then it col-
lapses to a whisper as she hears once more the knocking: "To
bed, to bed! There's knocking at the gate. Come, come, come,
come, give me your hand!" Reaching out, she seizes the hand
of somebody who isn't there and pulls him from the stage as
she had done in II ii. But the new turn of her final phrase
shows her full subconscious recognition of the reality of their
defeat. She used to say firmly to him: "What's done is done."
(III ii 14) Now she says wistfully, "What's done cannot be
undone."

The scene now shifts to one group of physical agents of
retribution and order, those Scottish lords who have deserted
Macbeth and now march "To give obedience where 'tis truly
owed," i.e. to Malcolm and the "English pow'r" that is to gather
near Birnam Wood not far from Macbeth's castle. Inside the
castle, Macbeth faces the worst. It is a strange mixture of man
we see here, a breaking-up in a way more terrible than we saw
in scene i with Lady Macbeth. He reminds himself that "The
spirits that know/All mortal consequences" have told him that
"No man that's born of woman" can harm him and that he

"cannot taint with fear" until Birnam Wood move on Dunsinane. What has he to fear, he says pathetically like the boy whistling through the graveyard, and yet almost immediately after saying that he reviles his servant for no reason except the boy's justifiable fear of the numbers of English soldiers. He screams for his armor-bearer, Seyton, and then sinks immediately into a gloomy cataloguing of how meaningless his life is. His poignant understanding of what old age should bring—"honor, love, obedience, troops of friends"—makes worse his (and our) recognition of what it has brought to him. But the gloom falls away as quickly as it came, and the frenzy is on him again: "I'll fight till from my bones my flesh be hacked. / Give me my armor." There is no need for it yet, but he puts it on and takes it off, and issues orders to the winds. He asks the Doctor how Lady Macbeth is and almost ignores the reply as he muses on his own troubled spirit. The whole scene testifies to the enormity of the mental and physical horror closing in on him, which he sees with a blinding and yet disbelieving clarity.

The rest of Act V plays out the bloody retribution. One by one, Macbeth's props fall. Malcolm tells each soldier to "hew him down a bough" from Birnam Wood to camouflage the size of the army. Macbeth's troops continue to desert him, but still he boasts: "Our castle's strength/Will laugh a siege to scorn." Lady Macbeth takes her own life, to which Macbeth can respond only with a numbed, almost gruesome comment that, after all, she had to die sometime. The "moving grove" descends on Dunsinane, and Macbeth, despite the anguish of every breath —"I 'gin to be aweary of the sun,/ And wish th' estate o' th' world were now undone"—still clings to life, to what he knows in his heart is "th' equivocation of the fiend,/That lies like truth." Like the bear at the stake, he must "fight the course," and he does so even when he learns from Macduff the crowning mockery of the fiend—that Macduff was "untimely ripped . . . from his mother's womb." In a final desperate assertion of will he cries, "Lay on, Macduff,/And damned be him that first cries 'Hold, enough!' " Macduff slays him, and retribution is complete. Dismembered Evil is brought before the true king, Malcolm, in the form of the "usurper's cursèd head" upon a pike, and order is restored as the rightful heir of Duncan announces in the final lines of the play that "What's more to do . . . We will perform in measure, time, and place." Nevertheless, a man greater than any of them is gone, and though the stage is full, there is, as always at the close of tragedy, an emptiness, a loss, that hurts.

STUDY QUESTIONS

ESSAY QUESTIONS

1. Take as your lead any of the following comments on *Macbeth* and write a paper developing the idea, or qualifying it, or refuting it—or a combination of all three:

   (a) "Macbeth may be seen in his wife, who has no name but his. They are bound in a terrible sympathy, each being to the other not only (in Macbeth's phrase) the 'dearest partner of greatness' but of fallen grace. The two of them are but man-and-woman variations on the blank desire for evil, the inexplicable negative principle, the frequent insanity that believes the will can change the very pattern of nature."

   (b) "... the essential struggle is in Macbeth's mind. . . . [he] is his own antagonist, and fights a doomed battle not only against the world but against himself. To balance having a villain-hero . . . the other characters in the play are well-meaning and decent, so that the usual Shakespeare conception of tragedy—a hero basically better than the world he lives in—is turned upside down. Morally considered, the play is nevertheless more than a melodrama because the villain *is* the hero, who suffers more from his own vice than from external retribution."

   (c) "*Macbeth* is a terrible play because its business is to give us some notion of what that damnation is which man embraces when he is, indeed, man enough for it. . . ."

   (d) "That the man who breaks the bonds that tie him to other men, who 'pour[s] the sweet milk of concord into Hell' is at the same time violating his own nature and thwarting his own deepest needs, is something that the play dwells on with a special insistence."

(e) "Macbeth's speech ('Tomorrow, and tomorrow, and to-morrow') has to be taken not as cynical, not as insightful, but rather as bitterly self-conscious. We can accept his despair as the logical, perhaps inevitable, reaction to his own life. To see life as 'signifying nothing' is accurate, so long as we understand that it is Macbeth's life that has become meaningless. Life in general remains unchallenged."

(f) "If you want to know the truth about Lady Macbeth's character, she hasn't one. There never was no such person. She says things that will set people's imagination to work if she says them in the right way: that is all."

(g) "When you play Shakespeare, don't worry about the character, but go for the music. It was by word music that he expressed what he wanted to express; and if you get the music right, the whole thing will come right. And neither he nor any other musician wrote music without *fortissimi*, and thundering ones too. It is your second rate people who write whole movements for muted strings and never let the trombones and the big drum go. It is not by tootling to him *con sordino* that Lady Macbeth makes Macbeth say, 'Bring forth men children only.' She lashes him into murder."

(h) "Macbeth himself is as humane in his reflections as he is inhumane in his acts. . . . he is a moralizing villain, but his moralizing is not clever aphoristic display. It comes from his heart. . . . We cannot view him with cold objectivity as something strange and apart. The unnaturalness of his acts is always counterpoised by the naturalness of his actions: his hesitant overtures to Banquo, his volubility after Duncan's death, his dazed petulance at the appearance of the ghost."

2. Show by a close analysis of the scenes with Macbeth and the weyard sisters that, while they know the future, they do not determine what Macbeth will do to bring about that future.

3. Take any scene that does not have either Macbeth or Lady Macbeth in it and discuss its function in the play. (If you choose Act V, consider all the scenes from which Macbeth or his wife is absent.) Deal with the scene (or scenes) as a contribution to the dramatizing of the order-disorder theme of the play.

4. In a recent film version of *Macbeth*, directed by Roman Polanski, the movie ends, not with Malcolm promising "measure, time, and place" in the kingdom, but with Donalbain out looking for the weyard sisters now that his brother is king. The suggestion is obvious and the irony heavy. Discuss what this directorial touch does for or to Shakespeare's *Macbeth*.

What grounds, if any, does the director have for including such a scene? What lines in Macduff's and Malcolm's final speeches does it render farcical?

5. Compare and contrast—in (a) characters, (b) atmosphere and tone, (c) structure of the action—*Macbeth* and *Julius Caesar* or *Macbeth* and *Hamlet*.

QUESTIONS

[*I i*]

1. One critic has called the short first scene an "overture," a term usually referring to the brief opening movement of a larger piece of music, using themes that will be developed fully in the body of the work. In what sense is scene i, then, an "overture"? What "themes" are suggested? What would be lost if the play opened with scene ii? Specifically, how does scene i affect our interest in scene ii?

2. If you did not know that the speakers were witches, would you recognize that they were evil powers by anything they say? Characterize *Evil* as it is revealed here. Consider, especially, lines 12-13. Why is their number three rather than two or four?

3. If you were directing the play, how would you stage this scene? How would you treat the witches so that for a modern audience they would not be simply comic Halloween figures? What sort of movements or choreography would you choose? What qualities would you want in the witches' voices? What would the witches wear and what stature would they be of? (Try acting out the scene with two classmates.)

[*I ii*]

1. The Captain, that "bloody man" of the King's opening question, is the first to describe Macbeth in battle. In what terms does he do so? what are Macbeth's opponents like? how does Macbeth handle them? against what kind of odds? with what kind of help? Characterize the language used and the man who uses it.

2. One director had the bleeding Captain whirled onto the stage, as if in a trance or daze, by the three witches. How might this alter our impression of what he says? Do the content

and manner of the Captain's speech support or contradict the idea that he is an instrument of the witches? State your evidence.

3. What more do we hear about the battle in Ross's report about Macbeth?

4. Is it significant that these two men of war give us our first impressions of Macbeth? Write a character sketch of the man as he is presented to us so far.

5. The King has little to say in the scene, but still we get a good picture of him. What kind of man is he? How do you know? What do you make of his response to the Captain's description of the dismembering of Macdonwald? Is it simply the response of an insensitive man who wants to hear the whole story before getting medical help for an obviously wounded man? In this world are there justifiable or "good" kinds of killings? If so, what would you say distinguishes them from "bad" kinds?

6. Scene ii begins to sketch out the nature of Good in the Good-Evil polarity that is developed in Act I. What is the nature of "Good" as revealed here? What suggestions are there that such "Good" carries the seeds of its opposite because of the kind of world in which it operates?

[*I iii*]

1. What is the dramatic value of turning immediately back to the witches in I iii rather than to Macbeth? How does the last line of I ii bring the witches to mind?

2. What kinds of business have the witches been up to since last we saw them? What seems to motivate their actions? What kinds of power do they have?

3. Account for Macbeth's response to the "All hails" of the witches as described by Banquo. How can you tell that Banquo's response is different from Macbeth's, even when the witches foretell the future for him? Consider lines 72-93. Why is his response different?

4. What advice would you give to an actor playing the part of Macbeth in this scene? How should he react (a) to each of the salutations beginning "All hail, Macbeth"? (b) to Banquo's question at 53-54? (consider line 59), (c) to the pronouncement in lines 67-69? How would you describe the difference in tone between Macbeth's speech in 72-81 and Banquo's in 82-83? After the witches vanish, what do you think needs special emphasizing and how would you suggest that an actor emphasize it?

5. Put in your own words lines 133-37, 142-50, and 151-54.
6. What further characteristics of Evil, as Shakespeare conceives it in this play, are revealed in this scene?

[*I iv*]

1. The King's lines at 13-16 are deeply ironic and prophetic, particularly since Macbeth enters immediately after they are spoken. In what sense are Malcolm's lines preceding his father's (3-12) equally ironic and prophetic?
2. This scene is loaded with indications of what characterizes Good in this world. Point them out. How would you counter the criticism that the protestations of loyalty and service on all sides in this scene ring false?
3. What images dominate the language in the scene? Why are they particularly appropriate in establishing the enormity of Macbeth's degeneration?
4. How do lines 56-61 tell us that much has happened in Macbeth's consciousness since the meetings with the witches? Compare the Macbeth of these lines with the one who speaks lines 151-54 in scene iii.
5. How does Shakespeare insure that in this scene Macbeth shall be constantly the object of the audience's attention? By what means does Shakespeare suggest visually the first beginnings of his isolation?

[*I v*]

1. When he wrote the letter, Macbeth did not know that Duncan intended to make Malcolm Prince of Cumberland, and there is nothing in the letter to suggest that he has had the thought of possibly murdering Duncan. And yet, Lady Macbeth's immediate reaction to the letter is her fear that he will not "catch the nearest way," which suggests that, to her, the "nearest" is the only way. What do we learn about her from the fact that she shows no surprise at what the letter says, but instead ponders his ability to bring about fulfillment of the outcome predicted by the witches?
2. How well does she know her husband? What has he said previously that supports or negates her assessment of him? What does she respect in him? What does she not respect?
3. How would you direct an actor to speak each of the brief lines Macbeth has in this scene (64-65, 67, 79)? He is not without ability to be voluble, even eloquent, as we have

already seen. What do his terseness and Lady Macbeth's volubility here suggest about what is going on in their minds?

4. Lady Macbeth speaks of pouring her "spirits" into his ear.
   What is the nature of her "spirits"? What is her attitude
   toward "fate and metaphysical aid" (29)? How does it differ
   from her husband's? Is there any evidence that the powers
   that she invokes to dehumanize her have already done so?
   Characterize the language and imagery of her invocation to
   the "murd'ring ministers."

5. Macbeth says of the "air-drawn dagger" (in II i) that it
   "marshall'st me the way that I was going" (50). In what sense
   do both the witches and Lady Macbeth only "marshall" him
   the way he was already going? In what sense do they influence him?

[*I vi*]

1. Scene vi shifts again to the world Duncan dominates and
   defines. What further attributes of that world are shown here?
   Consider especially lines 1-11 and contrast them with I v
   42-54.

2. Duncan is a gracious and generous king, as his language and
   his acts show. Is he also a foolish one? As onlookers, we
   know that he invites his own bloody end by going to Inverness, and the irony of almost every word uttered here and in
   scene iv is extreme. Is there any reason why he should act
   or believe otherwise than he does?

3. Why is it significant that Banquo enters the castle in company with Duncan and that he echoes the King's comments
   about the "pleasant seat" the castle has?

4. In what way is it visually suggestive that Lady Macbeth leads
   the group into the castle?

[*I vii*]

1. Scene v opens with Lady Macbeth reading her husband's letter and then eagerly wishing him there to carry out their
   "fell purpose." She has no misgivings, no imaginative fore-
   taste of the possible consequences. Scene vii opens with
   Macbeth alone, revealing a vast difference of mood and
   imagination. Write out his soliloquy in your own words, or
   reconstruct the line of reasoning. How would you answer the
   argument that he is not really wrestling with conflicting
   values, but simply engaging in some reassuring rationalizing
   —that he fully intends to go through with the murder, but

likes to think of himself as an essentially noble man driven to the deed by lack of proper recognition of his talents and deservings?

2. What reasons does he give Lady Macbeth for wanting to "proceed no further in this business"? How do they differ from the ones he gave himself? Why the difference?

3. How does she handle his wavering? Do her responses to his arguments deal with what he's saying or do they shift the ground? Where is he vulnerable?

4. What is gruesomely prophetic about his rejoinder to her taunts: "I dare do all that may become a man;/Who dares do more is none" (50-51)? What seems to be *her* definition of manhood? What is his?

[*II i*]

1. What does Shakespeare gain by having Banquo and Fleance appear at this time? Are Banquo's comments in lines 8-11 simply general remarks about wanting a peaceful night's sleep or do they express something more? What might be some of the "cursèd thoughts" that he dreads? How would you stage this seemingly neutral encounter to suggest the disquiet and tension the two men feel as they parry verbally? Remember that as soon as Macbeth is alone, the "air-drawn dagger" appears; obviously the tautness is in him all during the conversation with Banquo. How might the appearance of the two torches be made suggestive? the use of Banquo's sword? Do you see anything prophetic in the fact that Banquo appears with his son and Macbeth with a servant?

2. How would you handle the matter of the dagger that Macbeth sees? Since he sees it *before* he speaks, how will he convey the experience to us? What value might there be if his behavior here were recognizably like his behavior on being accosted by the weyard sisters? What action should take place at line 41?

3. Account for the difference between the first half of his soliloquy (lines 41-57) and the second half (57-72). Read the lines aloud several times. The tone of 41-57 is highly charged, almost frenzied; that of 57-72 is detached, almost trance-like, ending in the matter-of-fact numbness of "I go, and it is done. The bell invites me./Hear it not, Duncan, for it is a knell/That summons thee to heaven, or to hell."

4. Considering the emphasis in the speech on kinds of motion— "stealthy pace," "ravishing strides," "moves like a ghost,"

"my steps which way they walk"—how do you think the actor should manage the movements toward Duncan's room?

[*II ii*]

1. Though most of the blood in *Macbeth* flows offstage and is only talked about or carried in on hands and daggers, it remains a powerful substance. Why? How are we kept conscious of it during and after the murder of Duncan?

2. Consider the change that has come over Lady Macbeth, starting with the first chink in her armor, her insistence that had Duncan "not resembled/My father as he slept, I had done't." (14-15) Do you think she means what she says? Why or why not?

3. Note how many references Macbeth makes to "sleep." What do you make of his single-minded concern with sleep and prayer? What is ironic about Lady Macbeth's comment in lines 64-66? What values does sleep seem to stand for in this play? Consider lines 43-48.

4. To what extent is Lady Macbeth's ability to act determined by her husband's inability? In other words, what indications are there that she has to summon reserves of will power to carry through the deed? What is shown about her state of mind by the fact that she does not see the daggers till line 57? To give this belated discovery credibility, *we* must not see them till she suddenly calls attention to them. How might the two actors of the parts achieve this result?

5. Can it be argued that each knock comes at the psychologically right moment? What is their cumulative effect?

[*II iii*]

1. We have spoken in the notes of the porter who jokes about Hell in the midst of a man-made hell. Put in your own words what purposes you think are served by this seemingly out-of-tune episode.

2. To what extent is the Macbeth we see in this scene different from the overwrought man of the previous scene? What does this outward change suggest about an inward change? Why did he kill the grooms? Why does he say that he killed them? Are his reasons taken at face value? How do you know?

3. We have no way of knowing whether Lady Macbeth's faint is genuine (the first onset of what will eventually destroy her) or simply a quick-witted gambit to take attention from her husband. What is your opinion? What evidence do you base it on?

4. Put lines 99-108 in your own words. What is ironic and prophetic about them? How does their very eloquence compound
the irony? Does Macbeth sense that they are ironic and
prophetic? Explain.

5. Why do Malcolm and Donalbain decide to leave at once?
Has Macbeth expected this? How do Macduff and Banquo
react to the discovery of the murder? Why are they not so
eloquent as Macbeth? How could Banquo's silence after Macbeth's entrance be made expressive for the audience? Where
should he direct his eyes when he finally does speak?

6. If you were staging this scene, how would you underscore
the overplaying by Macbeth, the apprehension of Duncan's
sons, the suspicions of Macduff and Banquo?

7. Trace carefully, step by step, the rising excitement and intensity of the scene. Where would you locate its climax? Why?

[*II iv*]

1. What lines in II iii are echoed by what the Old Man and Ross
have to report in this scene? What is the purpose of attaching
to the murder all these unnatural happenings?

2. Do you suppose that Macduff believes all that he says to Ross
(27-35)? What suggests that he doesn't?

3. What central theme is emphasized in the last line of the
scene? Is the Old Man being intentionally ironic in this last
speech? Discuss.

[*III i*]

1. What do you take to be the meaning of Banquo's speech
(1-10)? Do you think it implies a vigilant prudence? Or an
opportunist's willingness to wait and see what profit can be
made from his knowledge? How aware do you think Banquo
is of the Macbeths' crime?

2. What qualities of character does Macbeth reveal in his interview with Banquo that have not been part of him before?
Consider the three questions he asks and the way he slips
them casually into the conversation. What does he need to
know?

3. Is there significance in the fact that Lady Macbeth leaves at
line 49 with the rest of the court? How does this resemble,
yet differ from, what happened in I vii? What is possibly
suggested by her going with no word of leave-taking?

4. In lines 54-79, Macbeth unburdens himself of his most immediate concerns. Why do his "fears in Banquo stick deep"?

At this point what does he mean by "safely thus" in line 54, "To be thus is nothing, but to be [i.e., unless I am] safely thus—"?

5. What does Macbeth reveal of himself in his treatment of the murderers? There can be no doubt that he is clever and resourceful as he bends them to his purpose, but how else might you describe one who mocks a man he has called "valor's minion" and "worthy gentleman" immediately before? Look carefully at his tactics, his language, and his reasonings. Why might it be fair to argue that he is really persuading *himself*, rationalizing what he is driven by his fears to do? Do you think he has convinced the murderers that Banquo was their enemy, or are they proceeding with the murder because they will be rewarded? Give evidence.

[*III ii*]

1. In Lady Macbeth's lines to herself at the beginning of scene ii (6-9) there is none of the fire and purposefulness that came in almost every speech before Duncan's murder. What has happened? What is the answer to her questions at line 10: "Why do you keep alone . . .?" and what is significant about this development in their relationship? Though they still speak endearingly to each other (lines 31-53), and she does her best to protect him at the banquet later on, on what grounds could it be argued that a radical change has, nevertheless, taken place?

2. Put lines 15-30 in your own words. How do they reinforce what Lady Macbeth has already said to herself as well as develop themes already introduced?

3. How does Macbeth's invocation of the powers of darkness ("seeling night") sum up all that has happened to him? Who formerly invoked them? Consider the language and images of lines 53-62 in determining what manner of man would dwell on such thoughts.

[*III iii*]

1. What purposes can you see for this brief scene showing the actual murder of Banquo and Fleance's escape? The result is reported to Macbeth as the banquet begins. Why isn't that sufficient? Consider the significance of the third murderer who was sent by Macbeth obviously as an afterthought and without any word to the two men he had originally persuaded

to do the job. What familiar aspect of tyrannical rule does this express?

2. Some critics have argued that the third murderer is Macbeth himself. Why is this an absurd suggestion? (Time is no problem.) Why did Macbeth hire others to do the killing in the first place?

[*III iv*]

1. Can it be said that in both appearances of the ghost Macbeth conjures it up and drives it away? In other words, what is on his mind or in his words each time the ghost appears and disappears, and how does the manifestation of the ghost, only to him and to the audience, represent to us his inner state at the feast?

2. One of the central themes of Act I was what it takes to become, or be, a man (I vii). How is that theme reflected in this scene? In what way are Macbeth's grounds for determining what a man is different here from what they were in Act I? Why is that difference significant?

3. This is the last we see of Lady Macbeth until the opening of Act V, when she is, in several respects, no longer part of the waking world. How much does she know of what Macbeth knows and imagines? How is her behavior throughout this scene consistent with what we saw in Acts I and II? How is it different?

4. Characterize Macbeth and Lady Macbeth as we see them after the guests leave. What kinds of thoughts are on his mind? He seems calm himself, but what is the nature of that calm? Why is it significant that he thinks almost immediately of Macduff's absence and of seeking out the weyard sisters "tomorrow"? Why is it significant that Lady Macbeth does not lecture him about his behavior now that they are alone and that she still has little idea of what he has done or plans to do?

5. Why are Macbeth's last words in the scene particularly ironic (168-70)? Consider the references to sleep and to being "yet but young in deed." Refer also to lines 93-95, 146-47, and 162-66.

6. If you were staging this scene, how would you handle the stage movement? Consider the importance of the banquet itself, the necessity of showing the Macbeths as hosts who have thoroughly defiled the idea of hospitality. Consider also the appearance of Banquo's ghost. How should he enter? What should he look like? (How do you know?) What should

he do? Also, would Lady Macbeth or any of the guests notice the First Murderer when he enters?

7. In some productions, Lady Macbeth almost pulls Macbeth offstage at the close of II ii, and this is echoed by having him almost pull her offstage after this scene. Would that echo be appropriate? Why or why not?

[*III vi*]

1. What signs are given us that an opposition to Macbeth is developing? What differences are noted here between the England of Edward and the Scotland of Macbeth? What differences between Edward and Macbeth?

2. Lennox tells *us* nothing that we did not already know. How then can the actor keep the speech from boring us? What purpose can he suggest to us that his irony has?

[*IV i*]

1. The choral scene which ends Act III affirms the inhumanity of the new king and of his rule. How is this affirmed more dramatically at the opening of Act IV? What connections are there here with I i? What is significant about the way the second witch refers to Macbeth just before he appears? about his attitude toward the witches at this point? about the fact that in his dealings with them now he does not *ask,* but *demands*? about the fact, too, that he now enters their domain?

2. Which of the apparitions tend to increase his confidence and why? Which tend to discourage him and why? Is there any reason why he should not react the way he does in each instance? Explain.

3. Put lines 160-72 in your own words. Compare this soliloquy with those in I vii 1-28 and II i 41-72. What differences in Macbeth are revealed? Would it be possible to interpret this scene up to this point as a way of rendering (in stage terms) a psychological state? If so, how would you account for the apparitions and the show of kings?

[*IV ii*]

1. Some critics have complained that this scene is overdone and unnecessary, that it is too obviously an attempt to drive home horror and elicit pity to be effective dramatically. Others have

argued that its presence is effective to bring home what the power of a man like Macbeth means, in "gut" terms, all the other murders having taken place either offstage or in darkness, and with the emphasis removed from the victim to the reactions of the criminal. What is your own view? What, if anything, do you think would be lost if the scene were omitted in production? what gained? Consider, in answering these questions, what goes on in scene iii.

2. What do you make of Ross's role here? He is the one who reports the murders to Macduff in England in the next scene, and he is in the forces that finally topple Macbeth, but up to this point he has remained outwardly loyal to him. Why does he show up at all here if there is nothing he can do to prevent the killings? He offers no more than the most vague kind of misgivings and fears. Remember, also, that a messenger shows up soon after he leaves to give a direct warning to Lady Macduff.

[IV iii]

1. This is by far the longest scene in the play, and some critics have called it talky and dull, a distracting interlude that is (a) badly conceived (the mutual testing being almost silly, the reference to King Edward simple flattery, and Ross's pussyfooting inexcusable) and (b) badly executed (the language is elocutionary, not dramatic, and the sudden, dragged-out conversation spoils the effect of Macbeth's rapid plunge into spiritual Hell). Give your reactions to these criticisms, either in part or as a whole.

2. What advice would you give to actors playing the parts of Malcolm and Macduff in this scene? The individual speeches are quite long. How would you prevent a static kind of recitation, counter-recitation effect? Is there anything in the *content* of Malcolm's speeches (58-113) that is likely to command the audience's attention? If so, what?

3. What do you take to be the point of the "Doctor" interlude (155-77)? Where else in the play do we find references to curative as opposed to destructive powers? In what ways may this be seen as part of the growing "opposition" to Macbeth?

4. How would you suggest handling the Malcolm-Macduff-Ross episode? Why does Ross lie when he first appears? Macduff never does answer Malcolm's misgivings earlier in lines 31-33. How does that fact color his reaction to Ross's revelations? How would you account for and handle Malcolm's harping on revenge rather than sympathy?

[V]

(Since Act V is made up of a series of short scenes, the questions will deal with the act as a whole.)

1. What words of Lady Macbeth repeat or suggest earlier ones spoken by her and her husband? What confusions of fact are there in her reenactment of past actions and comments? What purposes are served by these repetitions and confusions?

2. Why is it significant that Lady Macbeth, not Macbeth, sinks into madness and suicide? Shakespeare could have made Macbeth an onlooker in the sleep-walking scene. Why do you suppose that he didn't? Do you see any special pathos in Lady Macbeth's final speech? What have her relations with her husband become?

3. In what sense are Macbeth's own last hours, seemingly totally different from his wife's (he is all action in Act V, and he scorns suicide), not so different as the surface view suggests? Consider (a) ironic echoes of past words, attitudes, and actions, (b) whether his bustling has any clear purpose or is itself nightmare-like, a series of disconnected knee-jerk reactions, and (c) the fact that while he won't "play the Roman fool" and die on his own sword, his reason is not that he wants to live, but that he wants to take others with him before he is killed.

4. What purposes are served by the rapid scene-switching back and forth between the troops approaching Dunsinane and Macbeth? How would you handle all this movement if you were staging the play? What dramatic effects would you especially want to highlight?

5. Are lines 46-51 in scene iii about Macbeth or Lady Macbeth? Explain. What other references to disease and curing can you find in Act V? Show that health and disease are deeply involved as themes in the play.

6. How do lines 9-15 of scene v prepare the way for 19-28? What does "such a word" (18) refer to? How do Macbeth's comments here sum up the horror of his descent into Hell?

7. Does Macbeth in any sense redeem himself in your eyes? Does Lady Macbeth? What evidence is there that he is fully aware of what he has done to himself and that he recognizes the horror of it? Discuss.

8. Act V is said by actors to be the supreme test of the man who takes the role of Macbeth. Why is this so?

SHAKESPEARE AND HIS WORKS

William Shakespeare was born in the Warwickshire town of Stratford on April 23, 1564 (a guess based on the record of his baptism dated April 26) and died there on April 23, 1616. He was the eldest of six children of John and Mary (Arden) Shakespeare. His father was a successful glovemaker and trader in Stratford and for a time was active in local civic and political affairs, serving for a term as high bailiff, or chief administrative officer of the town; his mother was the daughter of a prosperous landowner. At age 18 he married Anne Hathaway, a woman some eight years his senior, by whom he had three children, Susanne in 1583, Hamnet and Judith (twins) in 1585.

Although he obviously spent most of his time in London between 1585 and 1611, he kept close ties with his home town, and his own family lived there throughout most of the year. In 1597 he purchased New Place, one of Stratford's finest homes, to which he retired in 1611.

There is no record of his formal schooling, but he undoubtedly attended the Stratford grammar school and got a solid grounding in Latin and literature since the masters during his school age years were Oxford graduates. When or why he went to London and turned to acting and writing plays is not known, but by 1592 he had clearly established a reputation in both fields; and for the next twenty years he turned out an average of almost two plays a year, plus a number of sonnets and several longer poems. He was a charter member of the Lord Chamberlain's Men, an acting company formed in 1594 (renamed the

King's Men in 1603), the foremost company of its time. He remained with the King's Men until his retirement. In 1599 the company moved into the newly built Globe Theater, in which Shakespeare had a financial interest. By that time, and for the rest of his life, he prospered financially through his acting-writing-investing ventures. More important, in his own time he was a widely respected and widely loved dramatist in an age that produced many and for an audience that understood and supported the theater.

ii

A chronological listing of Shakespeare's published works follows. There is no certainty about most of the assigned dates, and probably never will be. As we have indicated in the Textual Note, there was in Shakespeare's day little of the concern we have for the printing of play scripts, and most of the assigned dates for composition are the result of scholarly research and supposition based on both external and internal evidence that we here need only to recognize.

PLAYS

1588–93	*The Comedy of Errors*
1588–94	*Love's Labor's Lost*
1590–91	*2 Henry VI*
1590–91	*3 Henry VI*
1591–92	*1 Henry VI*
1592–93	*Richard III*
1592–94	*Titus Andronicus*
1593–94	*The Taming of the Shrew*
1593–95	*The Two Gentlemen of Verona*
1594–96	*Romeo and Juliet*
1595	*Richard II*
1594–96	*A Midsummer Night's Dream*
1596–97	*King John*
1596–97	*The Merchant of Venice*
1597	*1 Henry IV*
1597–98	*2 Henry IV*
1598 -1600	*Much Ado About Nothing*
1598–99	*Henry V*

1599	*Julius Caesar*
1599–1600	*As You Like It*
1599–1600	*Twelfth Night*
1600–1601	*Hamlet*
1597–1601	*The Merry Wives of Windsor*
1601–2	*Troilus and Cressida*
1602–4	*All's Well That Ends Well*
1603–4	*Othello*
1604	*Measure for Measure*
1605–6	*King Lear*
1605–6	*Macbeth*
1606–7	*Antony and Cleopatra*
1605–8	*Timon of Athens*
1607–9	*Coriolanus*
1608–9	*Pericles*
1609–10	*Cymbeline*
1610–11	*The Winter's Tale*
1611	*The Tempest*
1612–13	*Henry VIII*

POEMS

1592	*Venus and Adonis*
1593–94	*The Rape of Lucrece*
1593–1600	*Sonnets*
1600–1601	*The Phoenix and the Turtle*

Books, Records, Films

Further reading about Shakespeare's times, his theater, and the plays themselves is always valuable and enlightening. Suggested below is a short list of excellent books, most of which are in print in inexpensive editions. Also included is information about available recordings of the complete text of *Macbeth* and about films available on video, for rental or purchase.

Books

Books marked with an asterisk are available in inexpensive editions.

* Bentley, Gerald E. *Shakespeare: A Biographical Handbook*. New Haven: Yale University Press.
* Bradley, A. C. *Shakespearean Tragedy*. New York: Meridian Books.

  Campbell, O. J., and Edward G. Quinn. *The Reader's Encyclopedia of Shakespeare*. New York: Thomas Y. Crowell.

  Chambers, E. K. *William Shakespeare: A Study of Facts and Problems*. 2 vols. London: Oxford University Press.
* Dean, Leonard F. (ed.). *Shakespeare: Modern Essays in Criticism*. New York: Oxford University Press.
* Harbage, Alfred. *Shakespeare's Audience*. New York: Columbia University Press.
* Kernan, Alvin B. (ed.). *Modern Shakespearean Criticism*. New York: Harcourt Brace Jovanovich, Inc.
* Nagler, A. M. *Shakespeare's Stage*. tr. by Ralph Manheim. New Haven: Yale University Press.

Video

1948
Orson Welles, Jeanette Nolan, Dan O'Herlihy, Roddy McDowall, Robert Coote
111 minutes
Beta, VHS
Republic Pictures Home Video

1954
Maurice Evans, Dame Judith Anderson
black and white
103 minutes
Beta, VHS
Video Dimensions

1971
Directed by Roman Polanski
Jon Finch, Francesca Annis, Martin Shaw, Terence Baylor
139 minutes
Beta, VHS
RCA Columbia Pictures Home Video

1984
Directed by Sarah Caldwell
Philip Anglim, Maureen Anderman
148 minutes
Beta, VHS
Films for the Humanities

Audio Recordings

All recordings are released in both monaural and stereo; the text will differ in minor respects from that used in this edition.

Caedmon
Anthony Quayle, Gwen Ffrangçon-Davies
3 cassettes
LC67-740

Listen Pleasure
Alec Guinness, Old Vic Company
2 cassettes
ISBN 0-88646-037-9